Table of Contents

See inside back cover for a list of free video tutorials available on Go-Crafty.com

Family Resemblance Hats

Easy

SIZES
Child (Adult Woman, Adult Man).
Shown in all three sizes.

MATERIALS
Yarn (4)
For Solid Hat
• 7oz/200g, 328yd/300m of any worsted weight wool/alpaca blend yarn in Deep Teal
For Color-Blocked Hat
• 3½oz/100g, 164yd/150m of any worsted weight wool/alpaca blend yarn in Light Blue (A) and Periwinkle (B)
For Striped Hat
• 3½oz/100g, 164yd/150m of any worsted weight wool/alpaca blend yarn in Teal (A) and Green (B)

Needles
• One pair size 8 (5mm) needles, *or size to obtain gauge*

MEASUREMENTS
Circumference 18½ (19½, 20½)"/47 (49.5, 52)cm
Length (brim folded up) 8 (8½, 9½)"/20.5 (21.5, 23)cm

GAUGE
22 sts and 25 rows to 4"/10cm over elongated rib (unstretched) using size 8 (5mm) needles.
TAKE TIME TO CHECK YOUR GAUGE.

K1, P1 RIB
(over an odd number of sts)
Row 1 (RS) K1, *p1, k1; rep from * to end.
Row 2 P1, *k1, p1; rep from * to end.
Rep rows 1 and 2 for k1, p1 rib.

ELONGATED RIB
(over an odd number of sts)
Row 1 (RS) K1, *p1, k1 wrapping yarn twice around needle; rep from * to last 2 sts, p1, k1.
Row 2 P1, *k1, sl next st wyif, dropping extra wrap; rep from * to last 2 sts, k1, p1.
Rep rows 1 and 2 for elongated rib.

SOLID HAT
Cast on 101 (107, 113) sts. Work in k1, p1 rib for 2½ (3, 3)"/6.5 (7.5, 7.5)cm, end with a WS row.
Work in elongated rib until piece measures 8 (8½, 9)"/20.5 (21.5, 23)cm from beg, end with a WS row.

Shape Crown
Cont k1, p1 rib, working as foll:

For Adult Man's Size Only
Next row (RS) Dec 3 sts evenly across row—110 sts.
Work 1 row even.

Next row [K2tog, rib 20 sts] 5 times—105 sts.
Work 1 row even.
Next row [K2tog, rib 19 sts] 5 times—100 sts.
Work 1 row even.

For Adult Woman's Size Only
Next row (RS) [K2tog, rib 13 sts] 7 times, rib to end—100 sts.
Work 1 row even.

For Child's Size Only
Next row (RS) K2tog, rib to end—100 sts.
Work 1 row even.

For All Sizes
Next row (RS) [K2tog, rib 18 sts] 5 times—95 sts.
Next row and every WS row Work even.
Next row [K2tog, rib 17 sts] 5 times—90 sts.
Next row [K2tog, rib 16 sts] 5 times—85 sts.
Next row [K2tog, rib 15 sts] 5 times—80 sts.
Next row [K2tog] 40 times—40 sts.
Next row [K2tog] 20 times—20 sts.
Next row [K2tog] 10 times—10 sts.

FINISHING
Cut yarn, leaving long tail. Thread through rem 10 sts. Pull tog tightly and secure end. Sew back seam, sewing first 2½ (3, 3)"/6.5 (7.5, 7.5)cm from WS, so that seam does not show when folded up. Fold up brim.●

COLOR-BLOCKED HAT
With A, cast on 101 (107, 113) sts. Work same as solid hat until piece measures 7 (7½, 8)"/18 (19, 20.5)cm from beg, end with a WS row. Change to B, and complete as for solid hat.

STRIPED HAT
With A, cast on 101 (107, 113) sts. Work in k1, p1 rib for 2½ (3, 3)"/6.5 (7.5, 7.5)cm from beg, end with a WS row. Cont in elongated rib as foll:
Begin Stripe Pattern
[With A, work 4 rows. With B, work 4 rows] 4 times. With A, work 4 rows more. Cont with B and work even (if necessary) until pieces measures 8½ (9, 9½)"/21.5 (23, 24)cm from beg, end with a WS row. Complete as for solid hat.

Cabled Panels Hat

Intermediate

MATERIALS
Yarn (**5**)
- 3½oz/100g, 143yd/131m of any tweed bulky weight acrylic/wool/rayon blend yarn in Red

Needles
- One set (5) size 10 (6mm) double-pointed needles (dpn), *or size to obtain gauges*

Notions
- Cable needle (cn)
- Stitch marker

MEASUREMENTS
Circumference (slightly stretched)
15"/38cm*
Length 9"/23cm
*Hat will stretch to fit most

GAUGES
- 14 sts and 20 rnds to 4"/10cm over St st, using size 10 (6mm) needles.
- 16 sts (1 rep) to approx 3¾"/9.5cm over cable pat, slightly stretched, using size 10 (6mm) needles.
TAKE TIME TO CHECK YOUR GAUGES.

STITCH GLOSSARY
5-st FC Sl 3 sts to cn and hold to front, k2, k3 from cn.
6-st FC Sl 3 sts to cn and hold to front, k3, k3 from cn.
7-st FC Sl 4 sts to cn and hold to front, k3, k4 from cn.

CABLE PATTERN
(multiple of 16 sts)
Rnds 1–3 *P2, k5, p2, k7; rep from * around.
Rnd 4 *P2, k5, p2, 7-st FC; rep from * around.
Rnds 5–8 Rep rnd 1.
Rep rnds 1–8 for cable pat.

HAT
Cast on 64 sts. Divide sts evenly over 4 needles (16 sts on each needle). Join, taking care not to twist sts, and pm for beg of rnd. Knit 2 rnds.
Next rnd *K1, p1; rep from * around.
Rep last rnd until piece measures 3½"/9cm from beg.

Begin Cable Pattern
Working 16-st rep 4 times around, work rnds 1–8 of cable pat twice.

Shape Crown
Next dec rnd *P2, k1, k2tog, k2, p2, k3, k2tog, k2; rep from * around—56 sts.
Next 2 rnds *P2, k4, p2, k6; rep from * around.
Next rnd *P2, k4, p2, 6-st FC; rep from * around.
Next 6 rnds *P2, k4, p2, k6; rep from * around.
Next dec rnd *P2tog, k1, k2tog, k1, p2tog, k2, k2tog, k2; rep from * around—40 sts.
Next rnd *P1, k3, p1, 5-st FC; rep from * around.
Next rnd *P1, k3, p1, k5; rep from * around.
Next dec rnd *P1, k2tog, k1, p1, k2, k2tog, k1; rep from * around—32 sts.
Next 2 rnds *K2tog; rep from * around.
Cut yarn and draw through rem 8 sts. Pull tight and secure end.

FINISHING
Weave in ends. Block to measurements.•

Two-Tone Fair Isle Hat

Intermediate

MATERIALS

Yarn (4)
• 3½oz/100g, 196yd/180m of any worsted weight microfiber/nylon blend yarn in Green (MC)
• 1¾oz/50g, 98yd/90m of any worsted weight microfiber/nylon blend yarn in Light Green (CC)

Needles
• One size 7 (4.5mm) circular needle, 16"/40cm long, *or size to obtain gauge*
• One set (5) size 7 (4.5mm) double-pointed needles (dpn)

Notions
• Stitch marker

MEASUREMENTS

Brim circumference 20"/51cm
Length 10"/25.5cm

GAUGE

20 sts and 28 rnds to 4"/10cm over St st using size 7 (4.5mm) needles.
TAKE TIME TO CHECK YOUR GAUGE.

HAT

With MC, cast on 92 sts. Join, taking care not to twist sts, and pm for beg of rnd.
Rnds 1–8 *K2, p2; rep from * around.
Next inc rnd K6, M1, k11, [M1, k12, M1, k11] 3 times, M1, k6—100 sts.
Work 8 rnds in St st (k every rnd).

Begin Chart
Rnd 1 Work 4-st rep 25 times around. Cont to work chart in this way through rnd 24. Cut CC.
With MC, work in St st until piece measures 8"/20.5cm from beg.

Shape Crown
Note Change to dpn when sts no longer fit comfortably on circular needle.
Dec rnd 1 *K8, k2tog; rep from * around—90 sts.
Rnd 2 and all even rnds through rnd 14 Knit.
Dec rnd 3 *K7, k2tog; rep from * around—80 sts.
Rnds 4–14 Cont in this manner, dec'ing 10 sts every other rnd by working 1 less st each rep until 30 sts rem, end with a k rnd.
Dec rnd 15 *K1, k2tog; rep from * around—20 sts.
Dec rnd 16 *K2tog; rep from * around—10 sts.
Dec rnd 17 *K2tog; rep from * around—5 sts.
Cut yarn and pull through rem sts, draw up and secure.

FINISHING

Weave in ends. Block to measurements. With MC and CC, make a 2½"/6.5cm pompom and secure to top of hat.•

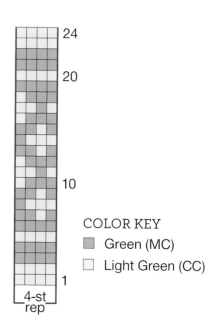

COLOR KEY
■ Green (MC)
□ Light Green (CC)

4-st rep

Garter Stripes Cap

Easy

MATERIALS

Yarn (4)
• 1¾oz/50g, 114yd/100m of any worsted weight wool yarn in Dark Teal (A), Medium Dark Teal (B), Medium Light Teal (C), and Light Teal (D)

Needles
• One each size 6 and 7 (4 and 4.5mm) circular needle, 16"/40cm long, *or size to obtain gauge*
• One set (4) size 7 (4.5mm) double-pointed needles (dpn)

Notions
• Stitch markers

MEASUREMENTS
Brim circumference 21"/53.5cm
Length 9"/23cm

GAUGE
20 sts and 44 rnds to 4"/10cm over garter st using larger needles.
TAKE TIME TO CHECK YOUR GAUGE.

CAP
With smaller circular needle and A, cast on 105 sts. Join, taking care not to twist sts, and pm for beg of rnd. Working in garter st (knit 1 rnd, purl 1 rnd), work in stripe sequence as foll:
12 rnds A, [2 rnds D, 2 rnds A] twice, 2 rnds D, 2 rnds C, 2 rnds D, 2 rnds C, 2 rnds B, 2 rnds C, 8 rnds B, 2 rnds D, 2 rnds B.
Change to larger circular needle.

With A, cont in St st (k every rnd) until piece measures 6"/15cm from beg, pm every 15 sts on last rnd—7 markers in total.

Shape Crown
Note Change to dpn when sts no longer comfortably fit on circular needle.
Dec rnd [K to 2 sts before next marker, k2tog] 7 times—7 sts dec'd.
Cont in St st, rep dec rnd every other rnd

13 times more—7 sts rem.
Cut yarn, pull through rem sts, draw up and secure.

FINISHING
Weave in ends. Block to measurements. Using all colors, make a 3"/7.5cm pompom and secure to top of hat.•

7

Lace Tam

Intermediate

MATERIALS

Yarn ❸
• 3½oz/100g, 228yd/200m of any DK weight merino wool yarn in Peach

Needles
• One each size 6 and 8 (4 and 5mm) circular needle, 16"/40cm long, *or size to obtain gauge*
• One set (5) size 8 (5mm) double-pointed needles (dpn)

Notions
• Removable stitch marker

MEASUREMENTS
Brim circumference (unstretched)
17"/43cm
Length 8½"/21.5cm

GAUGE
16 sts and 26 rnds to 4"/10cm over lace pat using larger needles.
TAKE TIME TO CHECK YOUR GAUGE.

LACE PATTERN
(multiple of 4 sts)
Rnd 1 *K2, yo twice, k2; rep from * around.
Rnd 2 *K2tog, (k1, p1) into the double yo, k2tog; rep from * around.
Rnd 3 *K4, yo twice; rep from * around.
Rnd 4 *[K2tog] twice, (k1, p1) into the double yo; rep from * around.
Rnd 5 Remove marker, k1, replace marker, *yo twice, k4; rep from * around.
Rnd 6 *(K1, p1) into the double yo, [k2tog] twice; rep from * around.
Rnd 7 Remove and replace marker 1 st to right (last st of previous rnd becomes first st of rnd), k3, yo twice, *k4, yo twice, rep from * around.
Rnd 8 *[K2tog] twice, (k1, p1) into the double yo; rep from * around.
Rep rnds 5–8 for lace pat.

NOTE
In lace pattern, beg of rnd moves one stitch to the left on rnd 5 and one stitch to the right on rnd 7. Use a removable stitch marker to keep track of beg of rnd.

TAM
With smaller circular needle, loosely cast on 88 sts. Join, taking care not to twist sts, and pm for beg of rnd.
Rnd 1 *K1, p1; rep from * around.
Rep rnd 1 for k1, p1 rib for 9 rnds more.
Next rnd Knit.
Next inc rnd [K4, M1] 22 times—110 sts.
Next rnd Knit.

Next inc rnd [K55, M1] twice—112 sts. Change to larger circular needle.

Begin Lace Pattern
Work in lace pat until piece measures 7½"/19cm from beg, end with a rnd 8.

Shape Crown
Note Change to dpn when sts no longer comfortably fit on circular needle.
Dec rnd 1 [K2tog] twice, *k2, [k2tog] twice; rep from * around—74 sts.
Rnd 2 Knit.
Dec rnd 3 *K2tog; rep from * around—37 sts.
Rnd 4 Knit.
Dec rnd 5 K1, *k2tog; rep from * around—19 sts.
Rnd 6 Knit.
Dec rnd 7 K1, *k2tog; rep from * around—10 sts.
Cut yarn, pull tail through rem sts, draw up and secure.

FINISHING
Weave in ends. Block to measurements. •

Jumbo Rib Hat

SIZES
Small/Medium (Large). Shown in size Small/Medium.

MATERIALS
Yarn ⑦
• 8¾oz/250g, 112yd/102m of any jumbo weight wool/acrylic/alpaca blend yarn in Yellow

Needles
• One size 15 (10mm) circular needle, 16"/40cm long, *or size to obtain gauge*
• One set (4) size 15 (10mm) double-pointed needles (dpn)

Notions
• One 5"/12.5cm faux-fur pompom
• Stitch marker

MEASUREMENTS
Brim circumference (unstretched)
15½"/39.5cm*
Length 9 (9¾)"/23 (24.5)cm
*Both sizes have same unstretched brim circumference, will stretch to fit

GAUGE
11 sts and 12 rnds to 4"/10cm in rib pat, unstretched, using size 15 (10mm) needle.
TAKE TIME TO CHECK YOUR GAUGE.

HAT
Cast on 42 sts. Join, taking care not to twist sts, and pm for beg of rnd.
Rnd 1 *K1, p1; rep from * around.
Rep rnd 1 for k1, p1 rib until piece measures 7½ (8¼)"/19 (21)cm from beg.

Shape Crown
Note Change to dpn when sts no longer comfortably fit on circular needle.
Dec rnd 1 *Ssk, k1, k2tog, p1; rep from * around—28 sts.

Next rnd Work even in pat.
Dec rnd 2 [K2tog] 14 times—14 sts.
Dec rnd 3 [K2tog] 7 times—7 sts.
Cut yarn, pull tail through rem sts, draw up and secure.

FINISHING
Weave in ends. Block to measurements. Secure pompom to top of hat.•

Cat Hat

MATERIALS

Yarn (4)
• 3½oz/100g, 217yd/198m of any worsted weight acrylic/wool/nylon blend yarn in Orange

Needles
• One each size 7 and 8 (4.5 and 8mm) circular needle, 16"/40cm long, *or size to obtain gauge*
• One set (4) each size 5 and 7 (3.75 and 4.5mm) double-pointed needles (dpn)

Notions
• Stitch markers

MEASUREMENTS

Brim circumference (unstretched)
18"/45.5cm*
Length (with brim folded)
8½"/21.5cm
*Will stretch to fit most

GAUGE

21 sts and 28 rnds to 4"/10cm over k3, p2, unstretched, using larger needles.
TAKE TIME TO CHECK YOUR GAUGE.

HAT

With larger circular needle, cast on 95 sts. Join, taking care not to twist sts, and pm for beg of rnd.
Rnd 1 *K3, p2; rep from * around.
Rep rnd 1 for k3, p2 rib for 2½"/6.5cm. Change to smaller circular needle and cont in k3, p2 rib until piece measures 10"/25.5cm from beg.

Shape Crown

Note Change to larger dpn when sts no longer comfortably fit on circular needle.
Dec rnd 1 *K1, k2tog, p2; rep from * around—76 sts.
Rnd 2 *K2, p2; rep from * around.
Dec rnd 3 *K2tog, p2; rep from * around—57 sts.
Rnd 4 *K1, p2; rep from * around.
Rnd 5 *K1, p2tog; rep from * around—38 sts.
Rnd 6 *K1, p1; rep from * around.
Dec rnd 7 *K2tog; rep from * around—19 sts.
Dec rnd 8 *K2tog; rep from * to last st, k1—10 sts.
Cut yarn, pull tail through rem sts, draw up and secure.

EARS (make 2)

With smaller dpn, cast on 11 sts. Work 8 rows in garter (k every row).
Row 1 (RS) K4, S2KP, k4—9 sts.
Row 2 and every WS row Knit.
Row 3 K3, S2KP, k3—7 sts.
Row 5 K2, S2KP, k2—5 sts.
Row 7 K1, S2KP, k1—3 sts.
Row 9 S2KP. Fasten off last st.

FINISHING

Weave in ends. Block to measurements. Using photo as guide, sew base of ears to sides of hat.
Fold brim approx 2½"/6.5cm to RS.●

Fair Isle Hat

● ● ●
Intermediate

MATERIALS

Yarn

• 3½oz/100g, 272yd/250m of any DK weight superwash wool in Taupe (A)
• 1¾oz/50g, 136yd/125m of any DK weight superwash wool in Red (B) and Gray (C)

Needles

• Two size 5 (3.75mm) circular needles, 16"/40cm long, *or size to obtain gauges*
• One set (5) size 5 (3.75mm) double-pointed needles (dpn)

Notions

• Scrap yarn
• Crochet hook size F (3.75mm)
• Stitch markers
• Tapestry needle

MEASUREMENTS

Head circumference 20"/51cm
Length 9½"/24cm

GAUGES

• 21 sts and 32 rnds to 4"/10cm over St st using size 5 (3.75mm) needles.
• 24 sts and 28 rnds to 4"/10cm over Fair Isle chart pat using size 5 (3.75mm) needles.
TAKE TIME TO CHECK YOUR GAUGES.

PROVISIONAL CAST-ON

Using scrap yarn and crochet hook, ch the number of sts to cast on plus a few extra. Cut a tail and pull the tail through the last chain. With knitting needle and yarn, pick up and knit the stated number of sts through the "purl bumps" on the back of the chain. To remove scrap yarn chain, when instructed, pull out the tail from the last crochet stitch. Gently and slowly pull on the tail to unravel the crochet stitches, carefully placing each released knit stitch on a needle.

NOTE

When working Fair Isle chart in rnds, work every rnd from right to left and bring new color from under the working color and twist yarns tog to prevent holes in work.

HAT

Beg at the inside hem edge of the hat, with circular needle and A, and using provisional cast-on method, cast on 105 sts. Join, taking care not to twist sts, and pm for beg of rnd. Work in St st (k every rnd) for 3½"/9cm.
Next inc rnd [K7, M1] 15 times—120 sts. Purl 1 rnd for turning ridge. Knit 2 rnds.

Begin Chart Pattern

Working the 8-st rep for 15 reps, work the chart pattern foll rnds 1–21. With A, work even in St st for 2 rnds. Then, before cont to knit, weave in all ends on the WS of the Fair Isle band. Slip all sts from provisional cast-on to spare circular needle and join the cast-on edge to form the doubled band as foll:
Folding the band at the turning ridge so that the purl sides are together, and with the cast-on edge at the inside, *[k1 st from the front needle and the back needle tog] 6 times, then k2 sts tog from front needle with 1 st from back needle; rep from * around—105 sts.
Cont with A only in St st until hat measures 9"/23cm from the turning ridge.

Shape Crown

Note Change to dpn when sts no longer comfortably fit on circular needle.
Dec rnd 1 [K1, k2tog, k16, ssk, pm] 5 times—95 sts.
Dec rnd 2 [K1, k2tog, k to 2 sts before marker, ssk] 5 times—10 sts dec'd.
Rep dec rnd 2 for 7 times more—15 sts rem. Cut yarn leaving a 12"/30.5cm end and thread on tapestry needle. Draw through sts on needle once, then draw through sts a 2nd time and pull up tightly to finish the top.

FINISHING

Weave in ends. Block to measurements. Make a 3½"/9cm pompom using all 3 colors and secure to top of hat.●

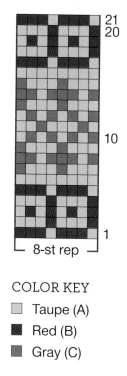

COLOR KEY

☐ Taupe (A)
■ Red (B)
▨ Gray (C)

Super Bulky Earflap Hat

MATERIALS

Yarn (6)
- 3½oz/100g skeins, 110yd/100m of any super bulky weight acrylic/wool/polyamide blend yarn in slightly variegated yarn

Needles
- One set (5) size 13 (9mm) double-pointed needles (dpn), *or size to obtain gauge*

Notions
- Crochet hook size L-11 (8mm)
- Stitch marker

MEASUREMENTS
Circumference (unstretched)
18"/45.5cm*
Length (before earflaps) 7"/17.5cm
*Hat will stretch to fit most

GAUGE
11 sts and 24 rnds to 4"/10cm over garter st using size 13 (9mm) needles.
TAKE TIME TO CHECK YOUR GAUGE.

HAT
Cast on 50 sts. Divide sts evenly over 4 needles (12–13–12–13). Join, taking care not to twist sts, and pm for beg of rnd. Work in garter st (p 1 rnd, k 1 rnd) until piece measures 4½"/11.5cm from beg, end with a p rnd.

Shape Crown
Dec rnd [K8, k2tog] 5 times—45 sts.
Next rnd Purl.
Dec rnd [K7, k2tog] 5 times—40 sts.

Next rnd Purl.
Cont in this manner, dec 5 sts every other rnd by working 1 less st each rep until 15 sts rem, end with a p rnd.
Next dec rnd [K1, k2tog] 5 times—10 sts.
Next rnd [P2tog] 5 times—5 sts.
Cut yarn, pull tail through rem sts, draw up and secure.

Right Earflap
With RS of cast-on edge facing, count 6 sts to the left of beg of rnd, then pick up and k 11 sts along cast-on edge.
Rows 1 and 2 Knit.
Row 3 K1, k2tog, k to last 3 sts, k2tog, K1.
Rep rows 1–3 three times more—3 sts rem.

Next row K3tog.
Transfer rem st to crochet hook. Make a chain 12"/30.5cm long. Fasten off.

Left Earflap
With RS of cast-on edge facing, count 17 sts to the right of beg of rnd, join yarn and pick up and k 11 sts along cast-on edge. Work as for right earflap.

FINISHING
Weave in ends. Block to measurements. Make one 2"/5cm pompom and two small ¾"/2cm pompoms. Secure the large pompom to top of hat and the small pompoms to end of ties.•

Seed Stitch Trim Hat

Easy

SIZES
Small/Medium (Large/X-Large).
Shown in size Large/X-Large.

MATERIALS
Yarn (5)
• 4oz/113g, 125yd/114m of any bulky weight wool/mohair blend yarn in Blue

Needles
• One each size 9 and 10 (5.5 and 6mm) circular needle, 16"/40cm long, *or size to obtain gauge*
• One set (5) size 10 (6mm) double-pointed needles (dpn)

Notions
• Stitch marker

MEASUREMENTS
Brim circumference 19 (21½)"/48 (54.5)cm
Length 8"/20.5cm

GAUGE
15 sts and 22 rnds to 4"/10cm over St st using larger needles.
TAKE TIME TO CHECK YOUR GAUGE.

SEED STITCH
(over an odd number of sts)
Rnd 1 *K1, p1; rep from * to last st, k1.
Rnd 2 *P1, k1, rep from * to last st, p1.
Rep rnds 1 and 2 for seed st.

HAT
With larger circular needle, cast on 71 (81) sts. Join, taking care not to twist sts, and pm for beg of rnd. Knit 4 rnds. Change to smaller circular needle.

Work 8 rnds in seed st. Change to larger circular needle.
Work in St st (k every rnd) until piece measures 6½"/16.5cm from beg, inc 1 st (dec 1 st) on last rnd—72 (80) sts.

Shape Crown
Note Change to dpn when sts no longer fit comfortably on circular needle.
For size Large/X-Large only
Next rnd *K8, k2tog; rep from * around—72 sts.

For both sizes
Rnds 1, 3, 5, & 7 Knit.

Rnd 2 *K7, k2tog; rep from * around—64 sts.
Rnd 4 *K6, k2tog; rep from * around—56 sts.
Rnd 6 *K5, k2tog; rep from * around—48 sts.
Rnd 8 *K4, k2tog; rep from * around—40 sts.
Cut yarn, pull tail through rem sts twice, draw up and secure.

FINISHING
Weave in ends. Block to measurements. Make a 3⅜"/8.5cm pompom and secure to top of hat.•

Half-Twist Ribbed Hat

Intermediate

SIZES
Adult Woman (Adult Man).
Shown in Adult Man.

MATERIALS
Yarn ❸
• 3½oz/100g, 225yd/205m of any
DK weight wool yarn in Bright Red

Needles
• One size 3 (3.25 mm) circular
needle, 16"/40cm long, *or size to
obtain gauge*
• One set (5) size 3 (3.25 mm) double-
pointed needles (dpn)

Notions
• Stitch marker
• Tapestry needle

MEASUREMENTS
Head circumference
19 (20)"/48 (51)cm
Length (slightly stretched)
8½"/21.5cm

GAUGE
30 sts and 30 rnds to 4"/10cm over
k1, p1 twisted rib (slightly stretched)
using size 3 (3.25mm) needle.
TAKE TIME TO CHECK YOUR GAUGE.

NOTE
Due to the elasticity of the ribbing, the
hat circumference will measure approx
2"/5cm smaller when the hat is laid flat.
It will stretch to fit when worn.

3-NEEDLE BIND-OFF
1) Hold right sides of pieces together on
two needles. Insert third needle knitwise
into first st of each needle, and wrap yarn
knitwise.
2) Knit these two sts together, and slip
them off the needles. *Knit the next two
sts together in the same manner.
3) Slip first st on 3rd needle over 2nd
st and off needle. Rep from * in step 2
across row until all sts are bound off.

HAT
With circular needle, cast on 144 (152)
sts. Join, taking care not to twist sts, and
pm for beg of rnd.
Rnd 1 *K1, p1; rep from * around.
Rnd 1 *K1 tbl, p1; rep from * around.
Rep these 2 rnds for k1, p1 twisted rib until
piece measures 2½"/6.5cm from beg.

Ridge Detail
Knit 1 rnd, purl 2 rnds, knit 1 rnd.

Then, cont in k1, p1 twisted rib until piece
measures 6½"/16.5cm from beg, end with
a rnd 1.

Shape Crown
Cont in k1, p1 twisted rib, change to dpn
and divide sts as foll:
Next rnd *Needle 1:* Rib 35 (37); *Needle 2:*
Rib 37 (39); *Needle 3:* Rib 35 (37); *Needle
4:* Rib 37 (39).
Dec rnd 1 *Needle 1:* SKP, work to the last
2 sts on needle, k2tog; *Needle 2:* P1, SKP,
work to the last 3 sts on needle, k2tog,
p1; *Needle 3:* Rep needle 1; *Needle 4:* Rep
needle 2—8 sts dec'd.
Dec rnd 2 *Needle 1:* SKP, work to the last
2 sts on needle, k2tog; *Needle 2:* P1, SKP,
work to the last 3 sts needle, k2tog, p1;
Needle 1: Rep needle 3; *Needle 4:* Rep
needle 2—8 sts dec'd.
Rep these 2 rnds until there are 7 sts on
needles 1 and 3, 9 sts on needles 2 and
4, for a total of 32 sts. Cut yarn, leaving a
long end.

FINISHING
Turn hat to the WS and divide sts over
2 needles. Join the top of hat using the
3-needle bind-off.
Weave in ends. Block to measurements.•

Messy Bun Hat

●●
Easy

MATERIALS

Yarn 🄢
• 1¾oz/50g, 98yd/90m of any bulky weight baby alpaca/bamboo blend yarn in Green

Yarn
• One size 10 (6mm) circular needle, 16"/40cm long, *or size to obtain gauge*

Notions
• Stitch marker

MEASUREMENTS
Head circumference 21"/53.5cm
Length 6¾"/17cm

GAUGE
16 sts and 26 rnds to 4"/10cm over double lace rib using size 10 (6mm) needle.
TAKE TIME TO CHECK YOUR GAUGE.

DOUBLE LACE RIB
(multiple of 6 sts)
Rnd 1 *K2, p1, yo, ssk, p1; rep from * around.
Rnd 2 *K2, [p1, k1] twice; rep from * around.
Rnd 3 *K2, p1, k2tog, yo, p1; rep from * around.
Rnd 4 Rep rnd 2.
Rep rnds 1–4 for double lace rib.

NOTE
Double lace rib may be worked from chart or text.

HAT
Cast on 84 sts. Join, taking care not to twist sts, and pm for beg of rnd.
Rnd 1 *K2, p2; rep from * around.
Rep rnd 1 for k2, p2 rib for 3 rnds more.
Work in double lace rib until piece measures 6"/15cm from beg, end with a rnd 2 or 4.
Next dec rnd *K2tog; rep from * around—42 sts.
Next 2 rnds *K1, p1; rep from * around.
Bind off in rib.

FINISHING
Weave in ends. Block to measurements.●

4
3
1

6-st rep

STITCH KEY
☐ knit
⊟ purl
🄾 yo
⊠ k2tog
⊠ ssk

Striped Toque

MATERIALS

Yarn (4)
• 1¾oz/50g, 122yd/112m of any worsted weight wool/nylon blend tweed yarn in Teal (A) and Moss (B)

Needles
• One set (4) size 8 (5mm) double-pointed needles (dpn), *or size to obtain gauge*
• One size 8 (5mm) circular needle, 16"/40cm long

Notions
• Stitch markers

MEASUREMENTS

Brim circumference (unstretched)
18"/45.5cm
Length 10"/25.5cm

GAUGE

18 sts and 31 rnds to 4"/10cm over St st using size 8 (5mm) needles.
TAKE TIME TO CHECK YOUR GAUGE.

NOTES

1) Toque is worked from top to brim.
2) Carry color not in use by twisting yarn with working color at beginning of every round.

TOQUE

With A and dpn, cast on 15 sts. Divide sts evenly over 3 needles. Join, taking care not to twist sts, and pm for beg of rnd. Knit 1 rnd.

Shape Crown

Rnd 1 *Kfb; rep from * around—30 sts.
Rnds 2–4 Knit.

Rep rnds 1–4 once more—60 sts.
Note Work sts onto circular needle during foll rnd.
Next rnd With B, *kfb; rep from * around—120 sts.
Knit 7 rnds.
[With A, knit 8 rnds; with B, knit 8 rnds] twice, with A, knit 3 rnds.
Next rnd With A, k25, pm, k10, pm, k50, pm, k10, pm, k25.

Shape Brim

Note Change to dpn if there are too few sts to comfortably fit on circular needle.
Next dec rnd [K to 2 sts before marker,

k2tog, sm, k to marker, sm, ssk] twice; k to end of rnd—4 sts dec'd.
Rep dec rnd 3 times more in color A, then 8 times in color B—72 sts.
With A, k 8 rnds. Bind off loosely.

FINISHING

Weave in ends. Block to measurements. With B, make a 2"/5cm pompom and secure tightly to top of hat.●

Textured Beret

MATERIALS

Yarn ❸
• 3½oz/100g, 142yd/130m of any light weight wool yarn in Peach

Needles
• One each size 7 and 9 (4.5 and 5.5mm) circular needle, 16"/40cm long, *or size to obtain gauge*
• One set (5) size 9 (5.5mm) double-pointed needles (dpn)

Notions
• Cable needle (cn)
• Stitch markers

MEASUREMENTS

Brim circumference (slightly stretched) 16"/40.5cm
Length 9"/23cm

GAUGE

16 sts and 22 rnds to 4"/10cm over St st using larger needles.
TAKE TIME TO CHECK YOUR GAUGE.

STITCH GLOSSARY

6-st RC Sl 3 sts to cn and hold to back, k3, k3 from cn.
8-st RC Sl 4 sts to cn and hold to back, k4, k4 from cn.

BERET

With smaller circular needle, cast on 68 sts. Join, taking care not to twist sts, and pm for beg of rnd.
Rnd 1 *K2, p2; rep from * around.
Rep rnd 1 for k2, p2 rib until piece measures 2"/5cm from beg.

Change to larger circular needle.
Next inc rnd [K16, kfb] 4 times—72 sts.
Next inc rnd [K1, kfb] 36 times—108 sts.

Begin Cable Pattern
Rnd 1 [K4, p10, k4] 6 times.
Rnd 2 and all even rnds Knit.
Rnd 3 [K1, M1, k2, ssk, p8, k2tog, k2, M1, k1] 6 times.
Rnd 5 [K2, M1, k2, ssk, p6, k2tog, k2, M1, k2] 6 times.
Rnd 7 [K3, M1, k2, ssk, p4, k2tog, k2, M1, k3] 6 times.
Rnd 9 [K4, M1, k2, ssk, p2, k2tog, k2, M1, k4] 6 times.
Rnd 11 Knit.
Rnd 13 [K6, 6-st RC, k6] 6 times.
Rnd 15 Knit.
Rnd 17 [K4, k2tog, k2, M1, p2, M1, k2, ssk, k4] 6 times.
Rnd 19 [K3, k2tog, k2, M1, p4, M1, k2, ssk, k3] 6 times.
Rnd 21 [K2, k2tog, k2, M1, p6, M1, k2, ssk, k2] 6 times.
Rnd 23 [K1, k2tog, k2, M1, p8, M1, k2, ssk, k1] 6 times.
Rnd 25 [K4, p10, k4] 6 times.

Shape Crown
Note Change to dpn when sts no longer comfortably fit on circular needle.
Rnd 26 K to last 4 sts, pm for new beg of rnd and remove previous marker.
Rnd 27 [8-st RC, p10] 6 times.
Rnd 28 Knit.
Dec rnd 29 K7, ssk, p8, k2tog, [k6, ssk, p8, k2tog] 4 times, k6, ssk, p8, pm for new beg of rnd (1 st will rem unworked, remove previous marker)—97 sts.
Dec rnd 30 K2tog, k to end of rnd—96 sts.

Rnd 31 [8-st RC, p8] 6 times.
Rnd 32 Knit.
Dec rnd 33 K7, ssk, p6, k2tog, [k6, ssk, p6, k2tog] 4 times, k6, ssk, p6, pm for new beg of rnd (1 st will rem unworked, remove previous marker)—85 sts.
Dec rnd 34 K2tog, k to end to rnd—84 sts.
Rnd 35 [8-st RC, p6] 6 times.
Rnd 36 Knit.
Dec rnd 37 K7, ssk, p4, k2tog, [k6, ssk, p4, k2tog] 4 times, k6, ssk, p4, pm for new beg of rnd (1 st will rem unworked, removed previous marker)—73 sts.
Dec rnd 38 K2tog, k to end of rnd—72 sts.
Rnd 39 [8-st RC, p4] 6 times.
Rnd 40 Knit.
Dec rnd 41 *[K2tog] 4 times, ssk, k2tog; rep from * 5 times—36 sts.
Dec rnd 42 [K2, k2tog] 9 times—27 sts.
Dec rnd 43 [K2tog] 13 times, k1—14 sts.
Cut yarn, pull tail through rem sts, draw up and secure.

FINISHING

Weave in ends. Block to measurements. •

3×3 Ribbed Hat

MATERIALS

Yarn

• 1¾oz/50g, 160yd/146m of any DK weight wool blend yarn in Gray (A), Green (B), and Cream (C)

Needles

• One size 6 (4mm) circular needle, 16"/40cm long, *or size to obtain gauge*
• One set (5) size 6 (4mm) double-pointed needles (dpn)

Notions

• Stitch marker

MEASUREMENTS

Brim circumference (unstretched) 19"/48cm

Length with brim folded 9"/23cm

GAUGE

25 sts and 32 rnds to 4"/10cm over k3, p3 rib, unstretched, using size 6 (4mm) needles.
TAKE TIME TO CHECK YOUR GAUGE.

HAT

With A, cast on 120 sts. Join, taking care not to twist sts, and pm for beg of rnd.
Rnd 1 *K3, p3; rep from * around.
Rep last rnd for k3, p3 rib for 4¼"/10.5cm. Cut A and join B.
With B, cont in k3, p3 rib until piece measures 8"/20.5cm from beg.

Shape Crown

Note Change to dpn when sts no longer comfortably fit on circular needle.
Dec rnd 1 *K3, p2tog tbl, p1, [k3, p3] 3 times, k3, p1, p2tog; rep from * around—112 sts.
Rnds 2–4 K the knit sts and p the purl sts.
Dec rnd 5 K3, p2tog tbl, [k3, p3] 3 times, k3, p2tog; rep from * around—104 sts.
Rnds 6–8 K the knit sts and p the purl sts.
Dec rnd 9 *K3, k2tog, k2, [p3, k3] twice, p3, k2, ssk; rep from * around—96 sts.
Rnds 10–12 K the knit sts and p the purl sts.
Dec rnd 13 *K3, k2tog, k1, [p3, k3] twice, p3, k1, ssk; rep from * around—88 sts.
Rnds 14–16 K the knit sts and p the purl sts.
Dec rnd 17 *K3, k2tog, [p3, k3] twice, p3, ssk; rep from * around—80 sts.
Rnds 18–20 K the knit sts and p the purl sts.
Dec rnd 21 *K3, p2tog tbl, p2, k3, p3, k3, p2, p2tog; rep from * around—72 sts.

Rnds 22–24 K the knit sts and p the purl sts.
Dec rnd 25 *K3, p2tog tbl, p1, k3, p3, k3, p1, p2tog; rep from * around—64 sts.
Rnd 26 K the knit sts and p the purl sts.
Dec rnd 27 *K3, p2tog tbl, k3, p3, k3, p2tog; rep from * around—56 sts.
Rnd 28 K the knit sts and p the purl sts.
Dec rnd 29 *K3, k2tog, k2, p3, k2, ssk; rep from * around—48 sts.
Rnd 30 K the knit sts and p the purl sts.
Dec rnd 31 *K3, k2tog, k1, p3, k1, ssk; rep from * around—40 sts.
Rnd 32 K the knit sts and p the purl sts.
Dec rnd 33 *K3, k2tog, p3, ssk; rep from * around—32 sts.
Rnd 34 K the knit sts and p the purl sts.
Dec rnd 35 *K3, p2tog tbl, p1, p2tog; rep from * around—24 sts.
Rnd 36 K the knit sts and p the purl sts.
Rnd 37 *K3, p3tog; rep from * around—16 sts.
Cut yarn, pull tail through rem sts, draw up and secure.

FINISHING

Weave in ends. Block to measuremnts. With C, make a 3½"/9cm pompom and secure to top of hat.
Fold brim approx 3"/7.5cm to RS.●

Blazing Fair Isle Hats

Intermediate

SIZES
Adult Woman (Adult Man). Shown in Adult Woman.

MATERIALS
Yarn (3)
• 1¾oz/50g balls, 136yd/125m of any DK weight superwash wool yarn in Fire Red (A), Burgundy (B), White (C), and Orange (D)

Needles
• One pair each size 3 and 6 (3.25 and 4mm) needles, *or size to obtain gauge*

Notions
• Eight stitch markers

MEASUREMENTS
Head circumference 20 (21)"/51 (53)cm
Length 8¼ (8¾)"/21 (22)cm

GAUGE
23 sts and 28 rows to 4"/10cm over St st using larger needles.
TAKE TIME TO CHECK YOUR GAUGE.

NOTES
Charts are worked in St st (k on RS, p on WS).

FIRE RED & ORANGE HAT
Beg at the lower edge with smaller needles and A, cast on 117 (125) sts.
Row 1 (RS) K1, *p1, k1; rep from * to end.
Row 2 P1, *k1, p1; rep from * to end.
Rep these 2 rows for k1, p1 ribbing for 9 (11) rows more.
Next row (WS) Work in rib and inc 6 (8) sts evenly spaced across—123 (133) sts. Change to larger needles and work even in St st (k on RS, p on WS) for 8 rows.

Begin Chart 1
Row 1 (RS) K1 (selvage st), work the 10-st rep of chart 12 (13) times, end with the last st of chart, then k1 (selvage st).
Cont to foll chart in this way through row 9. Then, cont with D, work even in St st until piece measures 5½ (5¾)"/14 (14.5)cm from beg, end with a RS row.

Shape Crown
Next row (WS) P2, [pm, p15 (16)] 8 times, p1 (3).
Dec row 1 (RS) [K to 2 sts before marker, SKP, sm] 8 times, end k2.
Rep dec row 1 every other row 6 (5) times more—67 (85) sts.
Dec row 2 (WS) P2, [sm, p2tog tbl, p to marker] 8 times, p to end.

Rep dec rows 1 and 2 for 3 (4) times more—11 (13) sts rem. Cut yarn.

FINISHING
Draw yarn through rem sts on needle once then draw through the same sts again and pull up tightly to secure.
Sew the back seam.
Steam block lightly to measurements.

BURGUNDY HAT
With smaller needles and D, cast on 117 (125) sts. Cut D and cont with B, work in k1, p1 rib as for Fire Red & Orange Hat for 11 (13) rows.
Next row (WS) Work in rib and inc 6 (8) sts evenly spaced across—123 (133) sts. Change to larger needles and cont in St st with B for 8 rows.

Begin Chart 2
Row 1 (RS) K1 (selvage st), work first st of chart, then work the 10-st rep of chart 12 (13) times, end k1 (selvage st).
Cont to foll chart in this way through row 11. Then, cont with B, work even in St st until piece measures 5½ (5¾)"/14 (14.5)cm from beg, end with a RS row.

Shape Crown
Work as for Fire Red & Orange Hat.

FINISHING
Work as for Fire Red & Orange Hat.•

CHART 1

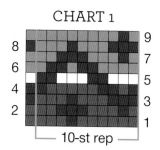

8 6 4 2
9 7 5 3 1
⌐ 10-st rep ⌐

CHART 2

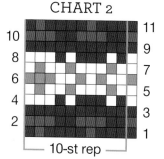

10 8 6 4 2
11 9 7 5 3 1
⌐ 10-st rep ⌐

COLOR KEY

▨ Fire Red (A)
▨ Burgundy (B)
☐ White (C)
▨ Orange (D)

Colossal Cables Hat

Easy

MATERIALS

Yarn (6)
• 3½oz/100g, 87yd/80m of any super bulky weight wool yarn in Purple

Needles
• One each size 10½ and 11 (6.5 and 8mm) circular needle, 16"/40cm long, *or size to obtain gauge*
• One set (4) size 11 (8mm) double-pointed needles (dpn)

Notions
• Stitch marker
• Cable needle (cn)

MEASUREMENTS

Brim circumference 18"/45.5cm*
Length 9"/23cm
*Brim will stretch to fit most

GAUGE

10 sts and 16 rnds to 4"/10cm over St st using size 11 (8mm) needle.
TAKE TIME TO CHECK YOUR GAUGE.

STITCH GLOSSARY

6-st LC Sl 3 sts to cn and hold to front, k3, k3 from cn.

HAT

With smaller needle, cast on 60 sts.
Row 1 *K2, p2; rep from * to end.
Join, taking care not to twist sts, and pm for beg of rnd.
Rnd 1 *K2, p2; rep from * around.
Rep rnd 1 for k2, p2 rib for 7 rnds more.
Change to larger needle.

Begin Cable Pattern
Rnds 1–5 *K6, p6; rep from * around.
Rnd 6 *6-st LC, p6; rep from * around.
Rep rnds 1–6 for cable pat until hat measures 7½"/19cm from beg, end with a rnd 5.

Shape Crown
Note Change to dpn when sts no longer comfortably fit on circular needle.
Dec rnd 1 *6-st LC, p2tog, p2, p2tog; rep from * around—50 sts.
Rnd 2 *K6, p4; rep from * around.
Dec rnd 3 *K6, [p2tog] twice; rep from * around—40 sts.

Rnd 4 *K6, p2; rep from * around.
Dec rnd 5 *K6, p2tog; rep from * around—35 sts.
Rnd 6 *K6, p1; rep from * around.
Rnd 7 *6-st LC, p1; rep from * around.
Rnd 8 *K2tog; rep from * to last st, k1—18 sts.
Cut yarn, pull tail through rem sts, draw up and secure.

FINISHING

Weave in ends. Block to measurements. Make a 3⅜"/8.5cm pompom and secure to top of hat.•

Tasseled Hat

Easy

MATERIALS

Yarn ④
- 3½oz/100g, 196yd/178m of any worsted weight alpaca/bamboo blend yarn in Blue

Needles
- Size 10½ (6.5mm) circular needle, 16"/40cm long, *or size to obtain gauge*
- One set (5) size 10½ (6.5mm) double-pointed needles (dpn)

Notions
- Tapestry needle
- Stitch markers
- One 5"/12.5cm length of cardboard

MEASUREMENTS

Head circumference (unstretched)
14½"/37cm*
Length to crown 9½"/24cm
*Will stretch to fit most

GAUGE

22 sts and 21 rnds to 4"/10cm over k1, p1 rib, unstretched, using size 10½ (6.5mm) needles.
TAKE TIME TO CHECK YOUR GAUGE.

HAT

Cast on 80 sts. Join, taking care not to twist sts, and pm for beg of rnd.
Rnd 1 *K1 tbl, p1; rep from * around.
Rep rnd 1 for twisted rib until piece measures 1½"/4cm from beg.
Next rnd *K1, p1; rep from * around.
Rep last round for k1, p1 rib until piece measures 7"/18cm from beg.

Shape Top

Dec rnd *Rib 14 sts, k2tog, pm; rep from * around—5 sts dec'd.
Next rnd K the knit sts and p the purl sts.
Dec rnd *Rib to 2 sts before marker, k2tog; rep from * around.
Rep last 2 rnds until 20 sts rem.
Work 1 rnd even.
Cut yarn, pull tail through rem sts, draw up and secure.

FINISHING

Weave in ends. Block lightly to measurements.

Tassel

Wrap yarn around 5"/12.5cm length of cardboard, leaving a 16"/40.5cm strand loose at either end. With a tapestry needle, knot both sides to the first loop and run the loose strand under the wrapped strands. Pull tightly and tie at the top. Cut the lower edge of the tassel and, holding the tassel about 1½"/4cm from the top, wind the top strands (one clockwise and one counterclockwise) around the tassel. Thread the two strands and insert them through the top of the tassel. Secure tassel to top of hat.•

Welted Hat

MATERIALS

Yarn 4
• 1¾oz/50g, 95yd/87m of any worsted wool yarn in Aquamarine (MC) and Pistachio (CC)

Needles
• One size 7 (4.5mm) circular needle, 16"/40cm long, *or size to obtain gauge*
• One size 5 (3.75mm) circular needle, 16"/40cm long
• One set (5) size 7 (4.5mm) double-pointed needles (dpn)

Notions
• Stitch marker

MEASUREMENTS

Brim circumference (unstretched)
16"/40.5cm
Length (unstretched) 6½"/16.5cm

GAUGE

19 sts and 24 rnds to 4"/10cm over St st using larger needles.
TAKE TIME TO CHECK YOUR GAUGE.

K1, P1 TWISTED RIB

(over an even number of sts)
Rnd 1 (RS) *K1 tbl, p1; rep from * to end.
Rep rnd 1 for k1, p1 twisted rib.

HAT

With MC and smaller needle, cast on 90 sts. Join, taking care not to twist sts, and pm for beg of rnd.
Work in k1, p1 twisted rib for 6 rnds.
Next inc rnd [K9, M1] 10 times—100 sts.

Begin Welts
Change to larger needle.
Rnd 1 With CC, knit.
Rnds 2–6 With CC, purl.
Rnds 7–10 With MC, knit.
Rep rnds 1–10 three times more, then work rnds 1–6 once more.
Cut CC and work in MC only to end.

Shape Crown
Note Change to dpn when sts no longer comfortably fit on circular needle.
Next dec rnd [K8, k2tog] 10 times—90 sts. Knit 1 rnd.
Next dec rnd [K7, k2tog] 10 times—80 sts. Knit 1 rnd.
Next dec rnd [K6, k2tog] 10 times—70 sts. Knit 1 rnd.

Next dec rnd [K5, k2tog] 10 times—60 sts. Knit 1 rnd.
Next dec rnd [K4, k2tog] 10 times—50 sts. Knit 1 rnd.
Next dec rnd [K3, k2tog] 10 times—40 sts. Knit 1 rnd.
Next dec rnd [K2, k2tog] 10 times—30 sts. Knit 1 rnd.
Next dec rnd [K1, k2tog] 10 times—20 sts. Knit 1 rnd.
Next dec rnd [K2tog] 10 times—10 sts. Knit 1 rnd.
Cut yarn, pull tail through rem sts, draw up and secure.

FINISHING

Weave in ends. Block to measurements.•

Fun with Faux Cables Hat

●● Easy

MATERIALS

Yarn (**4**)
• 3½oz/100g, 174yd/160m of any worsted weight wool yarn in Blue

Needles
• Size 9 (5.5mm) circular needle, 16"/40cm long, *or size to obtain gauge*
• One set (5) size 9 (5.5mm) double-pointed needles (dpn)

Notions
• Stitch marker

MEASUREMENTS

Circumference (unstretched)
16"/40.5cm*
Height 8"/20.5cm
*Will stretch to fit most

GAUGE

25 sts and 24 rnds to 4"/10cm over mock cable pat, slightly stretched, using size 9 (5.5mm) needles.
TAKE TIME TO CHECK YOUR GAUGE.

STITCH GLOSSARY

3-st right twist Skip 2 sts on LH needle, insert needle from front to back into the 3rd st on LH needle and knit it in front of the 2 skipped sts, knit the 2nd skipped st, then knit the 1st skipped st and drop all three sts from LH needle.

3-st right twist dec K2tog but do not drop from LH needle, k next st on LH needle then drop all three sts from LH needle—1 st dec'd.

MOCK CABLE PATTERN

(multiple of 5 sts)
Rnd 1–4 *K3, p2; rep from * around.
Rnd 5 *3-st right twist, p2; rep from * around.

Rnd 6 Rep rnd 1.
Rep rnds 1–6 for mock cable pat.

HAT

With circular needle, cast on 100 sts. Join, taking care not to twist sts, and pm for beg of rnd.
Rnd 1 *K1 tbl, p1; rep from * around.
Rep last rnd for twisted rib for 1¼"/3cm. Work in mock cable pat until piece measures approx 6"/15cm from beg, end with a pat rnd 5.

Shape Crown

Note Change to dpn when sts no longer fit comfortably on circular needle.
Rnd 1 [K3, p2, k3, p2tog] 10 times—90 sts.

Rnd 2 *K3, p2, k3, p1; rep from * around.
Rnd 3 [K3, p2, k2, ssk] 10 times—80 sts.
Rnd 4 *K3, p2, k3; rep from * around.
Rnd 5 [K3, p2, 3-st right twist dec] 10 times—70 sts.
Rnd 6 *K3, p2, k2; rep from * around.
Rnd 7 [K3, p2, k2tog] 10 times—60 sts.
Rnd 8 [K3, p2tog, k1] 10 times—50 sts.
Rnd 9 [K2, ssk, k1] 10 times—40 sts.
Rnd 10 [K2, ssk] 10 times—30 sts.
Rnd 11 [K3tog] 10 times—10 sts.
Cut yarn, pull tail through rem sts, draw up and secure.

FINISHING

Weave in ends. Block to measurements.●

Colorblock Hats

Easy

SIZES
Adult Small/Medium (Large/X-Large).
Shown in Large/X-Large.

MATERIALS
Yarn (6)
• 7oz/200g, 109yd/100m of any super bulky weight wool yarn in Blue (version 1 MC, version 2 CC) and Light Blue (version 1 CC, version 2 MC)

Yarn
• One each size 13 and 15 (9 and 10mm) circular needle, 16"/40cm long, *or size to obtain gauge*
• One set (5) size 15 (10mm) double-pointed needles (dpn)

Notions
• Stitch marker

MEASUREMENTS
Brim circumference (unstretched)
17 (19)"/43 (48)cm
Length 9"/23cm

GAUGE
9½ sts and 14 rnds to 4"/10cm over St st using larger needles.
TAKE TIME TO CHECK YOUR GAUGE.

NOTE
Two versions are shown. Choose one color for MC and one color for CC for version 1 and swap colors for version 2. Stripe patterns are different.

HAT
With smaller circular needle and MC, cast on 40 (45) sts. Knit 1 row.

Join, taking care not to twist sts, and pm for beg of rnd.
Purl 1 rnd, knit 1 rnd, purl 1 rnd.
*With CC, knit 1 rnd, purl 1 rnd.
With MC, knit 1 rnd, purl 1 rnd.
Rep from * once more.
Cut CC. Change to larger needle.

For Version 1 Only
Working in St st (k every rnd), work 6 rnds MC, 5 rnds CC, 5 rnds MC.

For Version 2 Only
Working in St st (k every rnd), work 9 rnds MC, 5 rnds CC, 2 rnds MC.

Shape Crown (Both Versions)
Note Change to dpn when sts no longer comfortably fit on circular needle.

Work in MC only to end.
Rnd 1 With MC, *k3, k2tog; rep from * around—32 (36) sts.
Rnds 2, 4, and 6 Knit.
Rnd 3 *K2, k2tog; rep from * around—24 (27) sts.
Rnd 5 *K1, k2tog; rep from * around—16 (18) sts.
Rnd 7 *K2tog; rep from * around—8 (9) sts.
Cut yarn, leaving a long tail, pull through rem sts twice, draw up and secure.

FINISHING
Weave in ends. Block to measurements. With one layer of MC and filling out rest with CC, make a 3⅜"/8.5cm pompom and secure to top of hat.•

Checkerboard Beanie

Easy

MATERIALS
Yarn (4)
• 1¾oz/50g, 115yd/105m of any worsted weight cotton/polyamide blend in Red (MC) and Green (CC)

Yarn
• One each size 6 and 7 (4mm and 4.5mm) circular needle, 16"/40cm long, *or size to obtain gauge*
• One set (5) size 7 (4.5mm) double-pointed needles (dpn)

Notions
• Stitch marker

MEASUREMENTS
Head circumference 18¼"/46.5cm
Length 7½"/19cm

GAUGE
21 sts and 34 rnds to 4"/10cm over checkerboard pat using larger needles.
TAKE TIME TO CHECK YOUR GAUGE.

K1, P1 RIB
(over an even number of sts)
Rnd 1 *K1, p1; rep from * around.
Rep rnd 1 for k1, p1 rib.

CHECKERBOARD PATTERN
(multiple of 8 sts)
Rnds 1–4 With CC, *k4, p4; rep from * around.
Rnds 5–8 With MC, *p4, k4; rep from * around.
Rep rnds 1–8 for checkerboard pat.

BEANIE
With MC and smaller circular needle, cast

on 96 sts. Join, taking care not to twist sts, and pm for beg of rnd. Work in k1, p1 rib for 1"/2.5cm.
Change to CC and larger circular needle, knit 1 rnd.
Begin Checkerboard Pattern
Beg with rnd 2, work checkerboard pat through rnd 8, then work rnds 1–8 for 4 times, then work rnds 1–4 once more.

Shape Crown
Note Change to dpn when sts no longer comfortably fit on circular needle.
Next dec rnd With MC, [p2tog, p2, k4, p4, k2, ssk] 6 times—84 sts.
Next rnd [P3, k4, p4, k3] 6 times.
Next dec rnd [P2tog, p1, k4, p4, k1, ssk] 6 times—72 sts.
Next rnd [P2, k4, p4, k2] 6 times.
Next dec rnd With CC, [k2tog, p4, k4, ssp] 6 times—60 sts.

Next rnd [K1, p4, k4, p1] 6 times.
Next dec rnd [P2tog, p3, k3, ssk] 6 times—48 sts.
Next rnd [P4, k4] 6 times.
Next dec rnd With MC, [k2tog, k2, p2, ssp] 6 times—36 sts.
Next rnd [K3, p3] 6 times.
Next dec rnd [K2tog, k1, p1, ssp] 6 times—24 sts.
Next rnd [K2, p2] 6 times.
Next dec rnd With CC, [p2tog, ssk] 6 times—12 sts.
Next rnd [P1, k1] 6 times.
Next dec rnd [K2tog] 6 times—6 sts.
Cut yarn, pull tail through rem sts, draw up and secure.

FINISHING
Weave in ends. Block to measurements. •

Baby Bonnets

Easy

BONNET

Top and Center Section

Cast on 16 sts. Work in garter st (k every row) for 10½"/26.5cm. Place 16 sts on a st holder.
Fold piece in half and place markers at each side of half-way fold.

First Side Section

With RS facing, beg at cast-on edge of Top and Center Section, pick up and k 24 sts along side edge to fold line marker. Pick up 1 st at marker and pm on this st (center st). Pick up and k 24 sts down rem side of Top and Center Section—49 sts.
Row 1 (WS) Knit to 1 st before marked center st, S2KP, k to end—2 sts dec'd.
Row 2 K to center st, p1 (center st), k to end.
Rep last 2 rows until 3 sts rem.
Last row K3tog. Fasten off last st.

Second Side Section

Work as for First Side Section along opposite side of Top and Center Section.

Neck Edging

With RS facing, pick up and k 60 sts along lower edge of bonnet (22 sts along one side edge, 16 sts on st holder, then 22 sts along second other side edge).
Row 1 (WS) K1, *p2, k2; rep from * to last 3 sts. p2, k1.

Row 2 K3, *p2, k2; rep from * to last st, k1.
Rep last 2 rows for k2, p2 rib for 1½"/4cm.
Bind off in rib.

Ties

With RS facing, pick up and k 8 sts along side of neck edging.
Work in garter st for 10½"/26.5cm.
Bind off.
Rep on opposite side of neck edging.

Brim (Optional)

If adding brim, pm along face edge of bonnet 2"/5cm from each side of Top and Center Section.
With RS facing, pick up and k 44 sts between markers.
Next row (WS) Purl.
Next row K1, k2tog, k to last 3 sts, ssk, k1—2 sts dec'd.
Rep last 2 rows 3 times more—36 sts.
Next row (WS–fold line) Knit.
Next row K1, M1, k to last st, M1, k1—2 sts inc'd.
Next row Purl.
Rep last 2 rows 3 times more—44 sts.
Bind off.
Fold brim along fold line and sew sides and bound-off edge in place.

FINISHING

Weave in ends. Block to measurements.●

Hound's Tooth Hat

● ● ●
Intermediate

MATERIALS
Yarn (4)
• 1¾oz/50g, 99yd/90m of any worsted weight wool/microfiber acrylic/cashmere blend yarn in Charcoal (A), Light Gray (B), and Green (C)

Needles
• One each size 7 and 8 (4.5 and 5mm) circular needle, 16"/40 long, *or size to obtain gauge*
• One set (4) size 8 (5mm) double-pointed needles (dpn)

Notions
• Stitch marker

MEASUREMENTS
Brim circumference 19"/48cm
Length 8"/20.5cm

GAUGE
21 sts and 19 rnds to 4"/10cm over St st using larger needle.
TAKE TIME TO CHECK YOUR GAUGE.

HAT
With A and smaller needle, cast on 112 sts. Join, taking care not to twist sts, and pm for beg of rnd.
Rnd 1 *With A, k2; with C, k2; rep from * around.
Rnd 2 *With A, k2, with C, p2; rep from * around.
Rep rnd 2 for corrugated rib for 8 rnds more. Cut C. Change to larger needle.

Begin Chart
Rnd 1 Work 4-st rep 28 times around.

Cont to work chart in this way through rnd 4, then rep rnds 1–4 until piece measures 3½"/9cm from beg, end with a rnd 4.

Shape Crown
Note Change to dpn when sts no longer comfortably fit on circular needle.
Cont in chart, work as foll:
Dec rnd 1 [K12, k2tog] 8 times—104 sts.
Rnd 2 and all even rnds to rnd 18 Work even in pat.
Cont to work in this manner, dec 8 sts every other rnd by working 1 less st each repeat until 32 sts rem.
Dec rnd 20 [K2, k2tog] 8 times—24 sts.
Dec rnd 21 [K1, k2tog] 8 times—16 sts.

Dec rnd 22 [K2tog] 8 times—8 sts.
Cut yarn, pull tail through rem sts, pull up and secure.

FINISHING
Weave in ends. Block to measurements. •

COLOR KEY
■ Charcoal (A)
□ Light Gray (B)

Textured Watch Cap

Easy

MATERIALS

Yarn (4)
- 3½oz/100g, 220yd/200m of any worsted weight wool yarn in Dark Aqua

Needles
- One size 6 (4mm) circular needle, 16"/40cm long, *or size to obtain gauge*
- One set (5) size 6 (4mm) double-pointed needles (dpn)

Notions
- Stitch marker

MEASUREMENTS
Head circumference 20"/51cm
Length (with folded brim) 8¼"/21cm

GAUGE
20 sts and 30 rnds to 4"/10cm over lozenge pat using size 6 (4mm) needles.
TAKE TIME TO CHECK YOUR GAUGE.

LOZENGE PATTERN
(multiple of 5 sts)
Rnd 1 *P4, k1; rep from * around.
Rnd 2 *P3, k2; rep from * around.
Rnd 3 *P2, k3; rep from * around.
Rnd 4 *P1, k4; rep from * around.
Rnd 5 *K1, p4; rep from * around.
Rnd 6 *K2, p3; rep from * around.
Rnd 7 *K3, p2; rep from * around.
Rnd 8 *K4, p1; rep from * around.
Rep rnds 1–8 for lozenge pat.

HAT
With circular needle, cast on 100 sts. Join, taking care not to twist sts, and pm for beg of rnd. Work in lozenge pat until piece measures 9"/23cm, end with a row 4.

Shape Crown
Note Change to dpn when sts no longer comfortably fit on circular needle.
Dec rnd 1 [K1, p2tog, p2, k1, p4] 10 times—90 sts.
Rnd 2 [K2, p2, k2, p3] 10 times.
Dec rnd 3 [K2, p2tog, k3, p2] 10 times—80 sts.
Rnd 4 [K7, p1] 10 times.
Dec rnd 5 [P1, k2tog, p4, k1] 10 times—70 sts.
Rnd 6 [P5, k2] 10 times.
Dec rnd 7 [P2tog, p2, k3] 10 times—60 sts.
Dec rnd 8 [P2tog, k4] 10 times—50 sts.
Rnd 9 [K1, p4] 10 times.
Dec rnd 10 [K2, p2tog, p1] 10 times—40 sts.
Rnd 11 [K3, p1] 10 times.
Dec rnd 12 [K2, k2tog] 10 times—30 sts.
Rnd 13 Knit.
Dec rnd 14 [K2tog] 15 times—15 sts.
Cut yarn, pull tail through rem sts, draw up and secure.

FINISHING
Weave in ends. Block to measurements. Make a 4"/10cm pompom and secure to top of hat.
Fold brim approx 2"/5cm to RS.●

Mitten Hat

MATERIALS
Yarn (3)
• 3½oz/100g, 228yd/208m of any DK weight wool yarn in Pink

Needles
• One size 6 (4mm) circular needle, 16"/40cm long, *or size to obtain gauge*
• One set (5) size 6 (4mm) double-pointed needles (dpn)

Notions
• Stitch markers

MEASUREMENTS
Head circumference 19"/48cm
Length 8½"/21.5cm

GAUGE
22 sts and 32 rows to 4"/10cm over St st and rib pat using size 6 (4mm) needles.
TAKE TIME TO CHECK YOUR GAUGE.

HAT
With circular needle, cast on 118 sts. Join, taking care not to twist sts, and pm for beg of rnd.
Rnd 1 *K1, p1; rep from * around.
Rep rnd 1 for k1, p1 rib for 1½"/4cm.
Next rnd [K17, k2tog] 6 times, k4—112 sts.
Next rnd Purl.

Begin Wide Rib Pattern
Rnd 1 [K11, p1, k1, p1] 8 times.
Rnd 2 [K11, p1, k 1 st in row below, p1] 8 times.
Rep rnds 1 and 2 for wide rib pat until piece measures 6½"/16.5cm from beg.

Shape Crown
Divide sts over 4 dpn as foll:
Dec rnd 1 *Needle 1*: Ssk, work 26 sts; *Needle 2*: Work 23 sts, k2tog, rib 3; *Needle 3*: Work same as *Needle 1*; *Needle 4*: Work same as needle 2—4 sts dec'd.
Rnd 2 Work even.
Dec rnd 3 *Needle 1*: Ssk, work to end of needle; *Needle 2*: Work to last 5 sts, k2tog, rib 3; *Needle 3*: Work same as needle 1; *Needle 4*: Work same as needle 2—4 sts dec'd.
Rnd 4 Work even.
Rep rnds 3 and 4 three times more—92 sts.
Next 14 rnds Rep dec rnd 3—36 sts with 9 sts on each needle.
Sl 18 sts from needles 1 and 2 to a strand of scrap yarn and sl rem 18 sts to the circular needle.

FINISHING
Turn the hat inside out and then sl the 18 sts from the scrap yarn back to one dpn. Then using 3-needle bind-off method with the 2 needles parallel, join the top of hat (see page 16 for 3-Needle Bind-Off instructions).
Weave in ends. Steam finished hat lightly on WS, turn to RS, and leave to dry.•

Cabled Hat

Intermediate

MATERIALS

Yarn (5)
- 3½oz/100g, 120yd/110m of any bulky weight acrylic/wool blend yarn in Teal (MC)
- 1¾oz/50g, 60yd/55m of any bulky weight acrylic/wool blend yarn in Orange (CC)

Needles
- One size 11 (8mm) circular needle, 16"/40cm long, *or size to obtain gauge*
- One set (4) size 11 (8mm) double-pointed needles (dpn)

Notions
- Stitch markers

MEASUREMENTS

Circumference 18–20"/45.5–51cm*
Length 9"/23cm
*Hat will stretch to fit most

GAUGE

12 sts and 18 rnds to 4"/10cm over k2, p2 ribbing, stretched, using size 11 (8mm) needles.
TAKE TIME TO CHECK YOUR GAUGE.

STITCH GLOSSARY

3-st FC Sl 2 sts to cn and hold to front, k1, k2 from cn.
3-st BC Sl 1 st to cn and hold to back, k2, k1 from cn.

With circular needle and MC, cast on 60 sts. Join, taking care not to twist sts, and pm for beg of rnd.
Rnd 1 *K2, p2; rep from * around.
Rep rnd 1 for k2, p2 rib for 4½"/11.5cm.

Begin Cable Pattern
Note Change to dpn when sts no longer comfortably fit on circular needle.
Dec rnd P2tog, p2, [pm, k6, pm, p2, p2tog, p2] 4 times, pm, k6, pm, p2—55 sts.
Cable rnd P to marker, *3-st FC, 3-st BC, p to marker; rep from *, end p2.
Next 3 rnds K the knit sts and p the purl sts.
Next rnd Rep cable rnd.
Next rnd K the knit sts and p the purl sts.
Dec rnd P1, p2tog [k6, p2tog, p1, p2tog] 4 times, k6, p2tog—45 sts.
Next rnd K the knit sts and p the purl sts.
Next rnd Rep cable rnd.
Next rnd K the knit sts and p the purl sts.
Dec rnd P2tog, [k6, p1, p2tog] 4 times, k6, p1—40 sts.
Next rnd K the knit sts and p the purl sts.

Next rnd Rep cable rnd.
Next rnd K the knit sts and p the purl sts, leaving last st unworked.
Dec rnd Sl last st from previous rnd to next needle, p2tog, *k6, p2tog; rep from * around—35 sts.
Next rnd K the knit sts and p the purl sts.
Next rnd Rep cable rnd.
Next rnd K the knit sts and p the purl sts.
Dec rnd *K2tog; rep from* to last st, k1—18 sts.
Cut yarn, pull tail through rem sts, draw up and secure.

FINISHING

Weave in ends. Fold up brim 1½"/4cm. With CC, make a 4"/10cm pompom and secure to top of hat.●

Lattice Hat

MATERIALS

Yarn

- 3½oz/100g, 206yd/280m of any size sock weight wool yarn in Yellow (A)
- 1¾oz/50g, 153yd/140m of any size sock weight wool yarn in Variegated Purple (B)

Needles

- One size 2 (2.75mm) circular needle, 20"/50cm long, *or size to obtain gauge*
- One set (5) size 2 (2.75mm) double-pointed needles (dpn)

Notions

- Stitch markers

MEASUREMENTS

- **Brim circumference** 20"/51cm
- **Length** 8"/20.5cm

GAUGE

32 sts and 34 rnds to 4"/10cm over St st and chart pat using size 2 (2.75mm) needles.
TAKE TIME TO CHECK YOUR GAUGE.

NOTES

1) Chart pat is worked in rounds in St st (k every rnd). Read all rnds from right to left.
2) When changing colors, twist yarns on WS to prevent holes in work. Carry color not in use loosely across WS.

HAT

With circular needle and A, cast on 160 sts. Join, taking care not to twist sts, and pm for beg of rnd.
Next rnd *K1, p1; rep from * around.
Rep last rnd for k1, p1 rib for 1½"/4cm.

Begin Chart 1

Rnd 1 Work 8-st rep 20 times around. Cont in chart pat as established until 10 rnds of chart have been worked 4 times (40 rnds total).

Shape Top

Note Change to dpn when sts no longer comfortably fit on circular needle.

Begin Chart 2

Rnd 41 Work 40-st rep 4 times around. Cont in chart pat as established, working S2KP dec as shown on chart, through row 64—8 sts.
Cut yarn, pull tail through rem sts, draw up and secure.

FINISHING

Weave in ends. Block to measurements.●

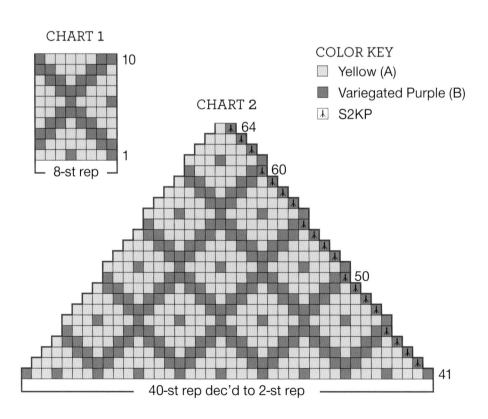

CHART 1

10

1

└ 8-st rep ┘

COLOR KEY
☐ Yellow (A)
◼ Variegated Purple (B)
⊼ S2KP

CHART 2

64

60

50

41

40-st rep dec'd to 2-st rep

Pumpkin Hat

● ●
Easy

SIZES
Baby (Child, Adult). Shown in Child's size.

MATERIALS
Yarn (4)
• 3½oz/100g, 170yd/156m of any worsted weight acrylic yarn in Orange (A)
• Small quantity of any worsted weight acrylic yarn in Green (B)

Needles
• One size 9 (5.5mm) circular needle, 16"/40cm long, *or size to obtain gauge*
• One set (5) size 9 (5.5mm) double-pointed needles (dpn)

Notions
• Stitch marker

MEASUREMENTS
Brim circumference 15 (17, 19)"/38 (43, 48)cm
Length (with brim rolled) 6 (6¾, 7½)"/15 (17, 19)cm

GAUGE
17 sts and 22 rnds to 4"/10cm over rib pat using size 9 (5.5mm) needles.
TAKE TIME TO CHECK YOUR GAUGE.

HAT
With circular needle and A, cast on 64 (72, 80) sts. Join, taking care not to twist sts, and pm for beg of rnd. Knit 6 rnds.

Begin Rib Pattern
Next rnd [K7, p1] 8 (9, 10) times.
Rep last rnd for rib pat until hat measures 5 (5¾, 6½)"/12.5 (14.5, 16.5)cm from beg with brim rolled.

Shape Crown
Note Change to dpn when sts no longer comfortably fit on circular needle.
Rnd 1 [K5, k2tog, p1] 8 (9, 10) times—56 (63, 70) sts.
Rnd 2 [Ssk, k4, p1] 8 (9, 10) times—48 (54, 60) sts.
Rnd 3 [K3, k2tog, p1] 8 (9, 10) times—40 (45, 50) sts.
Rnd 4 [Ssk, k2, p1] 8 (9, 10) times—32 (36, 40) sts.

Rnd 5 [K1, k2tog, p1] 8 (9, 10) times—24 (27, 30) sts.
Rnd 6 *Ssk, p1; rep from * to last st of rnd, sl last purl st to beg of rnd—16 (18, 20) sts.
Change to B.
Rnd 7 With B, [k2tog] 8 (9, 10) times—8 (9, 10) sts.
With B, knit 6 rnds even.
Next rnd *K2tog; rep from * to last 0 (1, 0) st(s), k0 (1, 0)—4 (5, 5) sts.
Cont in I-cord as foll:
*Knit one row. Without turning work, slide the sts back to the opposite end of needle to work next row from RS. Pull yarn tightly from the end of the row. Rep from * for 3"/7.5cm. Cut yarn and pull through rem sts, secure tail on inside of stem.
Tie an overhand knot in stem at last dec rnd.

FINISHING
Weave in ends. Block to measurements.●

Broken Rib Hat

Easy

MATERIALS

Yarn (5)
• 3½oz/100g, 120yd/110m of any bulky weight acrylic/wool blend yarn in Green

Needles
• One each size 9 and 10½ (5.5 and 6.5mm) circular needle, 16"/40cm long, *or size to obtain gauge*
• One set (4) size 10½ (6.5mm) double-pointed needles (dpn)

Notions
• Stitch marker

MEASUREMENTS
Circumference (unstretched) 18"/45.5cm
Length 8½"/21.5cm

GAUGE
12 sts and 18 rnds to 4"/10cm over broken rib, slightly stretched, using larger needle.
TAKE TIME TO CHECK YOUR GAUGE.

P2, K3, RIB
(multiple of 5 sts)
Rnd 1 *P2, k3; rep from * around.
Rep rnd 1 for p2, k3 rib.

BROKEN RIB
(multiple of 5 sts)
Rnd 1 *P1, k4; rep from * around.
Rnd 2 *P3, k2; rep from * around.
Rep rnds 1 and 2 for broken rib.

HAT
With smaller circular needle, cast on 60 sts. Join, taking care not to twist sts, and pm for beg of rnd. Work p2, k3 rib for 1½"/4cm. Knit 1 rnd.
Next inc rnd *K1, kfb; rep from * around—90 sts.
Change to larger circular needle and work in broken rib until piece measures 7"/18cm from beg, end with a pat rnd 1.

Shape Crown
Note Change to dpn when sts no longer comfortably fit on circular needle.
Dec rnd [P2tog, p1, k2] 18 times—72 sts.
Next rnd *P1, k3; rep from * around.
Dec rnd [P2tog, k2] 18 times—54 sts.
Next rnd *P1, k2, rep from * to end.
Dec rnd [P1, k2tog] 18 times—36 sts.
Dec rnd [K2tog] 18 times—18 sts.
Dec rnd [K3tog] 6 times—6 sts.
Cut yarn, pull tail through rem sts, draw up and secure.

FINISHING
Weave in ends. Block lightly to measurements.•

Zigzag Colorwork Hat

Intermediate

MATERIALS

Yarn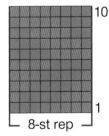
• 3½oz/100g hanks, 125yd/114m of any worsted weight wool yarn in Pink (A) and Gray (B)

Needles
• One size 8 (5mm) circular needle, 16"/40cm long, *or size to obtain gauge*
• One set (5) size 8 (5mm) double-pointed needles (dpn)

Notions
• Stitch marker

MEASUREMENTS
Brim circumference (unstretched)
18"/45.5cm
Length 8½"/21.5cm

GAUGE
17 sts and 22 rnds to 4"/10cm over St st and chart 1 using size 8 (5mm) needles.
TAKE TIME TO CHECK YOUR GAUGE.

NOTE
Charts are worked in St st (k every rnd).

HAT
With circular needle and A, cast on 80 sts. Join, taking care not to twist sts, and pm for beg of rnd.
Rnd 1 *K1, p1; rep from * around.
Cut A and join B.
Rnds 2–11 With B, *k1, p1; rep from * around.

Begin Chart 1
Rnd 1 Work 8-st rep 10 times around. Cont to work chart 1 in this way until rnds 1–10 have been worked twice, then work rnds 1–5 once more.

Begin Chart 2
Note Change to dpn when sts no longer comfortably fit on circular needle.
Rnd 1 Work 16-st rep 5 times around. Cont to work chart in this way through rnd 12—10 sts.
Cut yarn, pull tail through rem sts, draw up and secure.

FINISHING
Weave in ends. Block to measurements.•

COLOR KEY
◼ Pink (A)
◼ Gray (B)

STITCH KEY
☐ k
⧄ k2tog
⧅ SKP

CHART 1

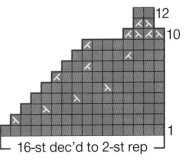

10

1

└ 8-st rep ┘

CHART 2

12

10

1

└ 16-st dec'd to 2-st rep ┘

Staggered Textures Hat

Easy

MATERIALS

Yarn (4)
• 3½oz/100g, 200yd/183m of any worsted weight wool yarn in Black (A), Charcoal (B), Blue (C), and Red (D)

Needles
• One size 7 (4.5mm) circular needle, 16"/40cm long, *or size to obtain gauge*
• One set (4) size 7 (4.5mm) double-pointed needles (dpn)

Notions
• Stitch marker

MEASUREMENTS
Brim circumference 20"/51cm
Length (with brim folded) 8"/20.5cm

GAUGE
22 sts and 26 rnds to 4"/10cm over k3, p3 rib using size 7 (4.5mm) needles.
TAKE TIME TO CHECK YOUR GAUGE.

HAT
With A and circular needle, cast on 108 sts. Join, taking care not to twist sts, and pm for beg of rnd.
Rnd 1 *K3, p3; rep from * around.
Rep last rnd for k3, p3 rib for 3"/7.5cm. Cut A and join B.
Next rnd With B, knit.

Begin Garter Rib
Rnd 1 With B, *p3, k3; rep from * around.
Rnd 2 *P1, k1, p1, k3; rep from * around.
Rep last 2 rnds until hat measures 7"/18cm from beg, end with a rnd 1. Cut B and join C.

With C, knit 1 rnd.
Rnd 1 *K3, p3; rep from * around.
Rnd 2 *K3, p1, k1, p1; rep from * around.
Rep last 2 rnds until hat measures 8¾"/22cm from beg, end with a rnd 1. Cut C. Join D and work to end as foll:

With D, knit 1 rnd.
Rnd 1 *P3, k3; rep from * around.
Rnd 2 *P1, k1, p1, k3; rep from * around.
Rep last 2 rnds 2 times more.

Shape Crown
Note Change to dpn when sts no longer comfortably fit on circular needle.
Dec rnd 1 *P3tog, k3, p3, k3; rep from * around—90 sts.
Rnd 2 *P1, k3, p1, k1, p1, k3; rep from * around.
Rnd 3 *P1, k3, p3, k3; rep from * around.
Rnd 4 Rep rnd 2.
Dec rnd 5 *P1, k3, p3tog, k3; rep from * around—72 sts.
Rnds 6, 7, and 8 *P1, k3; rep from * around.
Dec rnd 9 *P1, k3tog, p1, k3; rep from * around—54 sts.
Rnds 10, 11, and 12 *P1, k1, p1, k3; rep from * around.
Dec rnd 13 *P1, k1, p1, k3tog; rep from * around—36 sts.
Rnd 14 *K2tog; rep from * around—18 sts.
Cut yarn, pull tail through rem sts, draw up and secure.

FINISHING
Weave in ends. Block to measurements With B, make a 3"/7.5cm pompom and secure to top of hat.•

Polar Bear Hat

MATERIALS

Yarn
• 3½oz/100g, 180yd/165m of any worsted weight wool yarn in White (A)
• Small quantity of similar yarn in Black (B)

Needles
• One set (5) size 7 (4.5mm) double-pointed needles (dpn), *or size to obtain gauge*

Notions
• Removable stitch marker
• Tapestry needle

MEASUREMENTS
Circumference 18½"/47cm
Length 6½"/16.5cm

GAUGE
18 sts and 26 rnds to 4"/10cm over St st using size 7 (4.5mm) needles.
TAKE TIME TO CHECK YOUR GAUGES.

KITCHENER STITCH
Cut a tail at least 4 times the length of the edge that will be grafted together and thread through a tapestry needle. Hold needles together with right sides showing, making sure each has the same number of live stitches, and work as follows:
1) Insert tapestry needle purlwise through first stitch on front needle. Pull yarn through, leaving stitch on needle.
2) Insert tapestry needle knitwise through first stitch on back needle. Pull yarn through, leaving stitch on needle.
3) Insert tapestry needle knitwise through first stitch on front needle, pull yarn through, and slip stitch off needle. Then, insert tapestry needle purlwise through next stitch on front needle and pull yarn through, leaving this stitch on needle.
4) Insert tapestry needle purlwise through first stitch on back needle, pull yarn through, and slip stitch off needle. Then, insert tapestry needle knitwise through next stitch on back needle and pull yarn through, leaving this stitch on needle.
Repeat steps 3 and 4 until all stitches on both front and back needles have been grafted.

HAT
With A, cast on 84 sts. Divide sts evenly over 4 dpn (21 sts per needle), taking care not to twist sts, and pn for beg of rnd.
Rnd 1 *K2, p2; rep from * around.
Cont in rnds of k2, p2 rib for 6 rnds more. Then work in St st (k every rnd) until piece measures 5"/12.5cm from beg.

Shape Crown
Dec rnd 1 *Needle 1*: K2tog, k to last 2 sts, SKP; *Needles 2, 3 and 4*: Work same as needle 1—8 sts dec'd.
Rnd 2 Knit.
Rep last 2 rnds 3 times more—52 sts.
Next 2 rnds Rep dec rnd 1 twice more—36 sts.
Divide sts evenly over 2 dpn (18 sts per needle). Using tapestry needle, graft sts tog using kitchener st.

Ears (make 2)
With A and using 2 dpn to work back and forth in rows, cast on 4 sts.
Row 1 [Kfb] 4 times—8 sts.
Row 2 [Pfb] 8 times—16 sts.
Work 10 rows in St st (k on RS, p on WS).
Divide sts evenly over 2 dpn (8 sts per needle). Using tapestry needle, graft sts tog using kitchener st.

FINISHING
Embroidery
Using tapestry needle and B, embroider front center of hat foll hat chart, and then embroider center of ears foll ear chart (see photos for placement).

With A, wind several times around ear base to form a circle (see photos). Sew ear seam and secure to hat. Rep for 2nd ear.●

HAT CHART

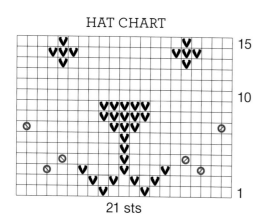

15

10

1

21 sts

EAR CHART

5

1

8 sts

STITCH KEY
V duplicate stitch
⊘ french knot

Winter Wonder Hat

Intermediate

MATERIALS

Yarn ⬤

• 8¾oz/250g, 123yd/112.5m of any super bulky weight wool yarn in Sherbet Green

Needles

• One size 15 (10mm) circular needle, 16"/40cm long, *or size to obtain gauge*
• One set (4) size 15 (10mm) double-pointed needles (dpn)

Notions

• Stitch marker

MEASUREMENTS

Brim circumference 18"/45.5cm*
Length (without earflaps) 9½"/24cm
*Brim will stretch to fit most

GAUGE

9 sts and 12 rows/rnds to 4"/10cm over St st using size 15 (10mm) needle.
TAKE TIME TO CHECK YOUR GAUGE.

STITCH GLOSSARY

M1R Insert LH needle from back to front under the horizontal strand between the stitch just worked and the next st on LH needle, knit this loop through the front—1 st inc'd.

M1L Insert LH needle from front to back under the horizontal strand between the stitch just worked and the next st on LH needle, knit this loop through the back—1 st inc'd.

HAT

Earflaps (make 2)
With dpn, cast on 3 sts.
Row 1 (WS) K1, p1, k1.

Row 2 K1, M1R, k1, M1L, k1—5 sts.
Row 3 K1, p to last st, k1.
Row 4 K1, M1R, k to last st, M1L, k1—2 sts inc'd.
Rows 5 and 7 Rep row 3.
Rows 6 and 8 Rep row 4.
Row 9 Rep row 3.
Row 10 Knit.
Rep last 2 rows 3 times more—11 sts.
Leave on hold on dpn.

Hat

With circular needle, cast on 7 sts, k across 11 sts of one earflap, cast on 11 sts, k across 11 sts of second earflap—40 sts. Join, taking care not to twist sts, and pm for beg of rnd.
Rnd 1 K18, p11, k11.
Rnd 2 Knit.
Cont in St st (k every rnd) until piece measures 7"/18cm after the earflaps have been worked.

Shape Crown

Note Change to dpn when sts no longer comfortably fit on circular needle.
Rnd 1 *K6, k2tog; rep from * around—35 sts.
Rnd 2 *K5, k2tog; rep from * around—30 sts.
Rnd 3 *K4, k2tog; rep from * around—25 sts.
Rnd 4 *K3, k2tog; rep from * around—20 sts.
Rnd 5 *K2, k2tog; rep from * around—15 sts.
Rnd 6 *K1, k2tog; rep from * around—10 sts.
Rnd 7 *K2tog; rep from * around—5 sts.
Cut yarn, pull tail through rem sts, draw up and secure.

FINISHING

Weave in ends. Block to measurements. Make two 3½"/9cm pompoms and one 4½"/11.5cm pompom. Secure larger pompom to top of hat and one smaller pompom to cast-on edge of each earflap.●

Classic Winter Hat

Easy

MATERIALS

Yarn (4)
• 3½oz/100g, 100yd/91m of any worsted weight alpaca/merino wool blend in Red (A) and Charcoal (B)

Needles
• One pair each size 10 and 10½ (6 and 6.5mm) needles, *or size to obtain gauge*

MEASUREMENTS
Head circumference 21"/53.5cm
Length (with brim folded) 10½"/27cm

GAUGE
16 sts and 20 rows to 4"/10cm over St st using larger needles.
TAKE TIME TO CHECK YOUR GAUGE.

HAT
With smaller needles and A, cast on 85 sts.
Row 1 (RS) K1, *p1, k1; rep from * to end.
Row 2 (WS) P1, *k1, p1; rep from * to end.
Rep rows 1 and 2 for k1, p1 rib until piece measures 5"/2cm from beg, end with a RS row.
Cut A, join B and k next row on WS, inc 3 sts evenly spaced across—88 sts.
Work in St st (k on RS, p on WS) for 2½"/6.5cm.
Change to larger needles and cont in St st until 5"/12.5cm have been worked in B, end with a WS row.

Shape Crown
Dec row (RS) [K5, k2tog, k4] 8 times—80 sts.
Work 3 rows even.
Dec row (RS) [K4, k2tog, k4] 8 times—72 sts.
Work 3 rows even.
Dec row (RS) [K3, k2tog, k4] 8 times—64 sts.
Work 1 row even.
Dec row (RS) [K3, k2tog, k3] 8 times—56 sts.
Work 1 row even.
Dec row (RS) [K3, k2tog, k2] 8 times—48 sts.
Work 1 row even.
Dec row (RS) [K2, k2tog, k2] 8 times—40 sts.
Work 1 row even.
Dec row (RS) [K2, k2tog, k1] 8 times—32 sts.

Work 1 row even.
Dec row (RS) [K1, k2tog, k1] 8 times—24 sts.
Work 1 row even.
Dec row (RS) [K1, k2tog] 8 times—16 sts.
Work 1 row even.
Cut yarn and draw through rem sts.

FINISHING
Sew back seam, reversing seam at ribbed edge so that it will not show when folded. Weave in ends. Block to measurements. With A, make a 2"/5cm pompom and secure to top of hat.•

Quartet of Cables Hat

Easy

MATERIALS

Yarn (4)
• 1¾oz/50g, 109yd/100m of any worsted weight merino blend tweed yarn in Blue (A)
• 3½oz/100g, 218yd/200m of any worsted weight merino blend tweed yarn in Cream (B)

Needles
• One each size 5 and 7 (3.75 and 4.5mm) circular needle, 16"/40cm long, *or size to obtain gauge*
• One set (4) size 7 (4.5mm) double pointed needles (dpn)

Notions
• Stitch marker
• Cable needle (cn)

MEASUREMENTS

Brim circumference 20"/51cm
Length (brim folded) 8¾"/22cm

GAUGE

19 sts and 28 rnds to 4"/10cm over rev St st using larger needles.
TAKE TIME TO CHECK YOUR GAUGE.

STITCH GLOSSARY

4-st LC Sl 2 sts to cn and hold to front, k2, k2 from cn.
6-st LC Sl 3 sts to cn and hold to front, k3, k3 from cn.

HAT

With smaller circular needle and A, cast on 112 sts. Join, taking care not to twist sts, and pm for beg of rnd.
Rnd 1 *K1, p1; rep from * around.
Rep rnd 1 for k1, p1 rib for 3"/7.5cm.
Cut A and join B. Change to larger circular needle.
Next rnd With B, p11, [k6, p22] 3 times, k6, p11.

Begin Cable Pattern
Rnd 1 P11, [6-st LC, p22] 3 times, 6-st LC, p11.
Rnds 2–7 P11, [k6, p22] 3 times, k6, p11.
Rep rnds 1–7 twice more, then rep rnds 1 and 2 once more.

Shape Crown
Note Change to dpn when sts no longer comfortably fit on circular needle.
Dec rnd 1 P9, p2tog tbl, [k6, p2tog, p18, p2tog tbl] 3 times, k6, p2tog, p9—104 sts.
Rnds 2, 4, and 8 Work in pats as established.
Dec rnd 3 P8, p2tog tbl, [k6, p2tog, p16, p2tog tbl] 3 times, k6, p2tog, p8—96 sts.
Dec rnd 5 P7, p2tog tbl, [k6, p2tog, p14, p2tog tbl] 3 times, k6, p2tog, p7—88 sts.

Rnd 6 P8, [6-st LC, p16] 3 times, 6-st LC, p8.
Dec rnd 7 P6, p2tog tbl, [k6, p2tog, p12, p2tog tbl] 3 times, k6, p2tog, p6—80 sts.
Dec rnd 9 P5, p2tog tbl, [k6, p2tog, p10, p2tog tbl] 3 times, k6, p2tog, p5—72 sts.
Dec rnd 10 P6, [SKP, k2, k2tog, p12] 3 times, SKP, k2, k2tog, p6—64 sts.
Rnd 11 P6, [4-st LC, p12] 3 times, 4-st LC, p6.
Dec rnd 12 P4, p2tog tbl, [k4, p2tog, p8, p2tog tbl] 3 times, k4, p2tog, p4—56 sts.
Rnds 13 and 15 Work in pats as established.
Dec rnd 14 P3, p2tog tbl, [k4, p2tog, p6, p2tog tbl] 3 times, k4, p2tog, p3—48 sts.
Dec rnd 16 P2, p2tog tbl, [k4, p2tog, p4, p2tog tbl] 3 times, k4, p2tog, p2—40 sts.
Rnd 17 P3, [4-st LC, p6] 3 times, 4-st LC, p3.
Dec rnd 18 P1, p2tog tbl, [k4, p2tog, p2, p2tog tbl] 3 times, k4, p2tog, p1—32 sts.
Rnds 19 and 21 Work in pats as established.
Dec rnd 20 P2tog tbl, [k4, p2tog, p2tog tbl] 3 times, k4, p2tog—24 sts.
Rnd 22 P1, [4-st LC, p2] 3 times, 4-st LC, p1.
Dec rnd 23 P1, [SKP, k2tog, p2] 3 times, SKP, k2tog, p1—16 sts.
Rnd 24 P1, [k2, p2] 3 times, k2, p1.
Rnd 25 [K2tog, SKP] 4 times—8 sts.
Cut yarn, pull tail through rem sts, draw up and secure.

FINISHING

Weave in ends. Block to measurements. Fold brim approx 2¼"/5.5cm to RS.•

Braided Cables Hat

Easy

MATERIALS

Yarn (5)
• 7oz/200g, 260yd/238m of any bulky weight acrylic/wool/nylon blend yarn in Yellow

Needles
• One pair size 10 (6mm) needles, *or size to obtain gauge*

Notions
• Cable needle (cn)

MEASUREMENTS
Head circumference 15"/38cm
Length 9¼"/23.5cm

GAUGE
21 sts and 24 rows to 4"/10cm over double cable pat using size 10 (6mm) needles.
TAKE TIME TO CHECK YOUR GAUGE.

STITCH GLOSSARY
6-st LC Sl 3 sts to cn and hold to front, k3, k3 from cn.
6-st RC Sl 3 sts to cn and hold to back, k3, k3 from cn.

K1, P1 RIB
(over an odd number of sts)
Row 1 (RS) K1, *p1, k1; rep from * to end.
Row 2 K the knit sts and p the purl sts.
Rep row 2 for k1, p1 rib.

DOUBLE CABLE PATTERN
(multiple of 11 sts plus 2)
Rows 1, 3, 9, and 11 (RS) *P2, k9; rep from * to last 2 sts, p2.
Row 2 and all WS rows K2, *p9, k2; rep from * to end.
Row 5 *P2, 6-st LC, k3; rep from * to last

2 sts, p2.
Row 7 *P2, k3, 6-st RC; rep from * to last 2 sts, p2.
Row 12 Rep row 2.
Rep rows 1–12 for double cable pat.

HAT
Cast on 79 sts. Work in k1, p1 rib for 2½"/6.5cm.

Begin Double Cable Pattern
Work rows 1–12 of double cable pat until piece measures 7½"/19cm from beg, end with a WS row.

Shape Crown
Next dec row (RS) *K3, k2tog; rep from

* to last 4 sts, k4—64 sts.
Purl 1 row, knit 1 row, purl 1 row.
Next dec row (RS) *K1, k2tog; rep from * to last 4 sts, k4—44 sts.
Purl 1 row, knit 1 row.
Next dec row (WS) *P1, p2tog; rep from * to last 2 sts, p2—30 sts.
Next row Knit.
Next dec row (WS) *P2tog; rep from * to end—15 sts.
Cut yarn, pull tail through rem sts, draw up and secure.

FINISHING
Sew back seam. Weave in ends. Block to measurements. Make a 4"/10cm pompom and secure to top of hat.•

Slouchy Pompom Hat

MATERIALS

Yarn (6)
• 3½oz/100g skeins, 110yd/100m of any super bulky weight acrylic/wool/polyamide blend yarn in Variegated Gray/Teal

Needles
• One size 11 (8mm) circular needle, 16"/40cm long, *or size to obtain gauge*
• One set (4) size 11 (8mm) double-pointed needles (dpn)

Notions
• Stitch markers

MEASUREMENTS

Circumference (above ribbed edge)
20"/51cm
Length 8½"/21.5cm

GAUGE

12 sts and 18 rnds to 4"/10cm over St st, slightly stretched, using size 11 (8mm) needles.
TAKE TIME TO CHECK YOUR GAUGE.

HAT

With circular needle, cast on 60 sts. Join, taking care not to twist sts, and pm for beg of rnd.
Rnd 1 *K2, p2; rep from * around.
Rep rnd 1 for k2, p2 rib for 3¼"/8cm.
Work in St st (k every rnd) until hat measures 6¾"/17cm from beg.

Shape Crown

Note Change to dpn when sts no longer comfortably fit on circular needle.
Dec rnd 1 [K2tog, k6, ssk] 6 times—48 sts.
Work 1 rnd even.
Dec rnd 2 [K2tog, k4, ssk] 6 times—36 sts.
Work 1 rnd even.
Dec rnd 3 [K2tog, k2, ssk] 6 times—24 sts.
Work 1 rnd even.
Dec rnd 4 [K2tog, ssk] 6 times—12 sts.
Dec rnd 5 [K2tog] 6 times—6 sts.
Cut yarn, pull tail through rem sts, draw up and secure.

FINISHING

Weave in ends. Block to measurements.
Make a 4" pompom and secure to top of hat.●

Long Earflap Hat

Intermediate

MATERIALS

Yarn
• 7oz/200g, 109yd/100m of any bulky weight acrylic yarn in Blue (MC) (5)
• 3½oz/100g, 69yd/63m of any super bulky weight polyester yarn in Blue and Red-Speckled (CC) (6)

Needles
• Two pair size 9 (5.5mm) needles, *or size to obtain gauge*

Notions
• Stitch holders
• Stitch marker

MEASUREMENTS
Head circumference 20"/51cm
Hat length 8½"/21.5cm
Earflap length 7¾"/20cm

GAUGE
15 sts and 29 rows to 4"/10cm over stripe pat using size 9 (5.5mm) needles.
TAKE TIME TO CHECK YOUR GAUGE.

SEED STITCH
(over an odd number of sts)
Row 1 (RS) K1, *p1, k1; rep from * to end.
Row 2 K the purl sts and p the knit sts.
Rep row 2 for seed st.

K1, P1 RIB
(over an even number of sts)
Row 1 (RS) *K1, p1; rep from * to end.
Row 2 K the knit sts and p the purl sts.
Rep row 2 for k1, p1 rib.

STRIPE PATTERN
Rows 1–10 With CC, knit.
Row 11 (RS) With MC, knit.
Row 12 With MC, purl.
Row 13 With MC, knit.
Row 14 With MC, purl.
Rep rows 1–14 for stripe pat.

LEFT EARFLAP
With MC, cast on 19 sts. Work in seed st until piece measures 7¼"/18.5cm from beg, end with a RS row.
Next inc row (WS) Work in seed st to end, cast on 2 sts—2 sts inc'd.
Next row (RS) Work even in seed st.
Rep last 2 rows once more—23 sts.
Leave sts on needle.

RIGHT EARFLAP
Work as for left earflap to increase row, end with a WS row.
Next inc row (RS) Work in seed st to end, cast on 2 sts—2 sts inc'd.
Next row (WS) Work even in seed st.
Rep last 2 rows once more—23 sts.
Leave sts on needle.

HAT
With MC, cast on 76 sts. Work in k1, p1 rib for 1½"/4cm, end with a WS row.

Join Earflaps
Note To join earflaps, hold needle with earflap sts (with RS facing) in front of working needle with hat sts. Insert third needle knitwise into first st on each needle and knit these two sts together. Cont to work in this way until earflap sts are joined.
Joining row (RS) K2, k next 23 sts tog with left earflap sts as described above, k26, k next 23 sts tog with right earflap sts as described above, k2.

Begin Stripe Pattern
Work rows 1–14 of stripe pat twice, then rep rows 1–10 once more.
Cut CC and cont in MC only to end.

Shape Crown
Next dec row (RS) With MC, [k7, k2tog] 8 times, k4—68sts.
Next row Purl.
Rep last 2 rows, dec 8 sts every other row by working 1 less st each repeat until 18 sts rem, end with a purl row.
Next dec row [K2tog] 9 times—9 sts.
Next row Purl.
Cut yarn, pull tail through rem sts, draw up and secure.
Sew back seam.

BRIM
With RS facing and MC, pick up and k 26 sts along front of hat above rib, between earflaps.
Next row (WS) Cut yarn leaving a tail, sl 5, join yarn, p16, turn.
Next row K17, turn.
Next row P18, turn.
Next row K19, turn.
Next row P20, turn.
Next row K21, turn.
Next row P22, turn.
Next row K23, turn.
Next row P24, turn.
Next row K25, turn.
Next row P26, turn.
Turning row (RS) Purl.
Next dec row (WS) Bind off 1 st, p to end.
Next dec row (RS) Bind off 1 st, k to end.
Rep last 2 rows 4 times more.
Bind off rem 16 sts.
Fold brim along turning row and sew in place.

FINISHING
Weave in ends. Block to measurements.•

Defined Lines Hat

● ●
Easy

MATERIALS

Yarns (4)
• 3½oz/100g, 210yd/192m of any worsted weight wool yarn in Dark Green (A) and Light Green (B)

Needles
• One size 8 (5mm) circular needle, 16"/40cm long, *or size to obtain gauge*
• One set (4) size 8 (5mm) double-pointed needles (dpn)

Notions
• Stitch marker

MEASUREMENTS
Brim circumference (unstretched)
20"/51cm
Length 8"/20.5cm

GAUGE
19 sts and 26 rnds to 4"/10cm over broken rib (unstretched) using size 8 (5mm) needles.
TAKE TIME TO CHECK YOUR GAUGE.

HAT
With A, cast on 96 sts. Join, taking care not to twist sts, and pm for beg of rnd.
Rnd 1 *K2, p2; rep from * around.
Rnd 2 K1, *p2, k2; rep from * to last 3 sts, p3, k1.
Rep rnds 1 and 2 for broken rib for 6 rnds more.

Cut A and join B. Cont in broken rib with B for 28 rnds.
Cut B and join A, work in A to end of hat.
Fold cast-on edge to WS and join hem as foll:
Hem joining rnd *Pick up loop from cast-on edge and place on LH needle, k tog with next st on needle; rep from * around.
With A, beg with a rnd 1, cont in broken rib for 28 rnds.

Shape Crown
Note Change to dpn when sts no longer comfortably fit on circular needle.

Dec rnd 1 *K2tog, p2; rep from * around—72 sts.
Rnd 2 *K1, p2; rep from * around.
Rnd 3 *K1, p2tog; rep from * around—48 sts.
Rnds 4 and 5 *K1, p1; rep from * around.
Rnd 6 *K2tog, p2tog; rep from * around—24 sts.
Rnd 7 *K2tog; rep from * around—12 sts.
Cut yarn, pull tail through rem sts, draw up and secure.

FINISHING
Weave in ends. Block to measurements.●

Parisian Cables Hat

Easy

MATERIALS

Yarn (4)
• 5¼oz/150g, approx 225yd/204m of any worsted weight cotton yarn in Plum (MC)
• 1¾oz/50g, approx 75yd/68m of any worsted weight cotton yarn in Orange (CC)

Needles
• One size 7 (4.5mm) circular needle, 16"/40cm long, *or size to obtain gauge*
• One set (5) size 7 (4.5mm) double-pointed needles (dpn)

Notions
• Cable needle (cn)
• Tapestry needle

MEASUREMENTS

Head circumference 19"/48.5cm
Length 8½"/21.5cm

GAUGE

30 sts and 31 rnds to 4"/10cm over cable pat using size 7 (4.5mm) needles.
TAKE TIME TO CHECK YOUR GAUGE.

STITCH GLOSSARY

6-st LC Sl 3 sts to cn and hold to front, k3, k3 from cn.

K2, P2 RIB

(multiple of 4 sts)
Rnd 1 *K2, p2; rep from * around.
Rep rnd 1 for k2, p2 rib.

HAT

With MC and circular needle, cast on 108 sts.

Join, taking care not to twist sts, and pm for beg of rnd. Work in k2, p2 rib for 7 rnds.
Next inc rnd *K3, M1; rep from * around—144 sts.

Begin Cable Pattern
Rnds 1–7 *K6, p3; rep from * around.
Rnd 8 *6-st LC, p3; rep from * around.
Rep rnds 1–8 until piece measures 7¼"/18.5cm from beg, end with rnd 8.

Shape Crown
Note Change to dpn when sts no longer comfortably fit on circular needle.
Next dec rnd [K6, p2tog, p1] 16 times—128 sts.
Next dec rnd [K6, p2tog] 16 times—112 sts.
Next dec rnd [K2tog, k2, k2tog, p1] 16 times—80 sts.

Next rnd [K4, p1] 16 times.
Next dec rnd [K1, k2tog, k1, p1] 16 times—64 sts.
Next dec rnd [K1, k2tog, p1] 16 times—48 sts.
Next dec rnd [K2tog, p1] 16 times—32 sts.
Next dec rnd [K2tog] 16 times—16 sts.
Cut yarn, pull tail through rem sts, draw up and secure.

FINISHING

Weave in ends. Block to measurements. With CC and tapestry needle, using photo as a guide, make French knots at the center of each cable, running a continuous thread up each cable to minimize ends. With CC, make 4"/10cm pompom and secure to top of hat.•

Welted Brioche Hat

Experienced

MATERIALS
Yarn (4)
• 1¾oz/50g, 82yd/75m of any worsted weight wool yarn in Green (MC) and Yellow (CC)

Needles
• One each size 6 and 7 (4 and 4.5mm) circular needle, 16"/40cm long, *or size to obtain gauge*
• One set (4) size 7 (4.5mm) double-pointed needles (dpn)

Notions
• Stitch marker

MEASUREMENTS
Brim circumference (unstretched)
19"/48cm
Length 9"/23cm

GAUGE
15 sts and 40 rows to 4"/10cm over two-color brioche rib using larger needle.
TAKE TIME TO CHECK YOUR GAUGE.

NOTE
Two-color brioche rib is reversible.

STITCH GLOSSARY
[k1 tog with yo] twice K1 st tog with yo; do not drop yo from LH needle. K next st tog with same yo, dropping yo from LH needle.

[p1 tog with yo] twice P1 st tog with yo; do not drop yo from LH needle. P next st tog with same yo, dropping yo from LH needle.

sl 2 p-sts with yo Bring yarn to front, slip next 2 purl sts to RH needle. When following sts are knit, yo will lay on top of the purl sts.

sl 2 k-sts with yo With yarn at front, slip next 2 knit sts to RH needle, wrap yarn over needle and around to front again. When following sts are purled, yo will lay on top of the knit sts.

TWO-COLOR BRIOCHE RIB
(multiple of 4 sts)
Rnd 1 With MC, *[k1 tog with yo] twice, sl 2 p-sts with yo; rep from * around.
Rnd 2 With CC, *sl 2 k-sts with yo, [p1 tog with yo] twice; rep from * around.
Rep rnds 1 and 2 for two-color brioche rib.

HAT
With smaller needle and MC, cast on 88 sts. Join, taking care not to twist sts, and pm for beg of rnd. Work around in k2, p2 rib for 10 rnds. Change to larger needle. Beg two-color brioche rib as foll:
Set-up rnd With MC, *k2, sl 2 p-sts with yo; rep from * around.
Work rnd 2 of two-color brioche rib, then rep rnds 1 and 2 twenty-three times, then rnd 1 once. Piece measure approx 5"/12.5cm from beg.

Shape Crown
Note Change to dpn when sts no longer comfortably fit on circular needle.
Next dec rnd With CC, *sl 2 k-sts with yo, p2tog with yo; rep from * around—66 sts.

Cont in two-color brioche rib as foll:
Rnd 1 With MC, *[k1 tog with yo] twice, sl 1 p-st with yo; rep from * around.
Rnd 2 With CC, *sl 2 k-sts with yo, p1 tog with yo; rep from * around.
Rep rnds 1 and 2 twelve times more.
Next dec rnd With MC, *k2tog with yo, sl 1 p-st with yo; rep from * around—44 sts.

Cont in two-color brioche rib as foll:
Rnd 1 With CC *sl 1 k-st with yo, p1 tog with yo; rep from * around.
Rnd 2 With MC, *k1 tog with yo, sl 1 p-st with yo; rep from * to end.
Rep rnds 1 and 2 three times more, then rnd 1 once.
Next dec rnd With MC, *sl 1 knitwise (k-st and its yo), k2tog (first p st on LH needle tog with next k st and its yo), psso, sl 1 p-st with yo; rep from * around—22 sts.
Next rnd With CC, *sl 1 k-st with yo, p1 tog with yo; rep from * around.
Next dec rnd With MC, [ssk] 11 times—11 sts.
Cut MC and CC leaving 8"/20.5cm tails. Thread MC through rem sts. Do *not* close opening.

FINISHING
I-cord Stem
With dpn and MC, cast on 3 sts leaving a long tail for sewing. Work I-cord as foll:
***Next row (RS)** With 2nd dpn, k3, do *not* turn. Slide sts back to beg of needle to work next row from RS; rep from * until piece measures 1"/2.5cm. Cut yarn leaving a long tail. Thread through rem sts. Pull tog tightly and secure.
With MC tail from top, sew running stitches around top opening. Insert stem halfway through top opening of hat. Pull tog tightly to close opening and fasten off, securing stem in place.•

Basket Weave Baby Hat

SIZES
Newborn (3 months, 6 months, 12 months). Shown in size 12 months.

MATERIALS
Yarn
• 5oz/141g, 242yd/222 of any DK weight acrylic yarn in Pink or Blue

Needles
• One pair each size 4 and 6 (3.5 and 4mm) needles, *or size to obtain gauge*

MEASUREMENTS
Brim circumference 12½ (13½, 15½, 16¾)"/32 (34.5, 39.5, 42.5)cm

GAUGE
22 sts and 30 rows to 4"/10cm over St st using larger needles.
TAKE TIME TO CHECK YOUR GAUGE.

HAT
With smaller needles, cast on 68 (74, 86, 92) sts. Work in St st (k on RS, p on WS) for 6 rows

Row 1 (RS) K2, *p1, k2; rep from * to end.
Row 2 P2, *k1, p2; rep from * to end.
Rep rows 1 and 2 for k2, p1 rib 3 times more. Change to larger needles.

Begin Border Pattern
Row 1 Knit.
Row 2 Purl.
Rows 3 and 5 K2, *p4, k2; rep from * to end.
Rows 4 and 6 P2, *k4, p2; rep from * to end.
Rows 7 and 8 Rep rows 1 and 2.
Rows 9 and 11 P3, k2, *p4, k2; rep from * to last 3 sts, p3.
Rows 10 and 12 K3, p2, *k4, p2; rep from * to last 3 sts, k3.
Rep rows 1–6 once more for border pat.

Next dec row (RS) Knit, dec 3 (0, 3, 0) sts evenly across—65 (74, 83, 92) sts.
Cont in St st until piece measures 4 (4¼, 4¾, 5)"/10 (11, 12, 13)cm from beg, end with a WS row.

Shape Crown
Next dec row (RS) K1, *k7, k2tog; rep from * to last st, k1—58 (66, 74, 82) sts. Purl 1 row. Knit 1 row. Purl 1 row.
Next dec row (RS) K1, *k6, k2tog; rep from * to last st, k1—51 (58, 65, 72) sts. Purl 1 row. Knit 1 row. Purl 1 row.
Next dec row (RS) K1, *k5, k2tog; rep from * to last st, k1—44 (50, 56, 62) sts. Purl 1 row.
Next dec row (RS) K1, *k4, k2tog; rep from * to last st, k1—37 (42, 47, 52) sts. Purl 1 row.
Next dec row (RS) K1, *k3, k2tog; rep

from * to last st, k1—30 (34, 38, 42) sts. Purl 1 row.
Next dec row (RS) K1, *k2, k2tog; rep from * to last st, k1—23 (26, 29, 32) sts. Purl 1 row.
Next dec row (RS) K1, *k1, k2tog; rep from * to last st, k1—16 (18, 20, 22) sts. Purl 1 row.
Cut yarn, pull tail through rem sts, draw up and secure.

FINISHING
Sew back seam, reversing for rolled bottom edge. Weave in ends.
Block to measurements.•

Brioche Beanie

Intermediate

SIZES
Small (Medium/Large). Shown in size Medium/Large.

MATERIALS
Yarn (4)
• 3½oz/100g, 186yd/170m of any worsted weight wool yarn in Blue

Needles
• One size 7 (4.5mm) circular needle, 16"/40cm long, *or size to obtain gauge*
• One set (4) size 7 (4.5mm) double-pointed needles (dpn)

Notions
• Stitch markers

MEASUREMENTS
Brim circumference (unstretched)
19¾ (22)"/50 (56)cm
Length 8½ (9)¾"/21.5 (23)cm

GAUGE
13 sts and 20 rnds to 4"/10cm over brioche rib, slightly stretched, using size 7 (4.5mm) needles.
TAKE TIME TO CHECK YOUR GAUGE.

STITCH GLOSSARY
Sl 1 k-st with yo With yarn in front, sl next k st purlwise to RH needle, wrap yarn over RH needle and around to front again.
Sl 1 p-st with yo With yarn in front, sl next p st purlwise to RH needle, wrap yarn over RH needle to back for yarn over, ready to work next knit st.
2-st decrease K2tog (next knit st with yarn over tog with foll p st), slip st back to LH needle, pass the foll k st with yarn over on LH needle over st and off needle, slip st back to RH needle—2 sts dec'd.

BEANIE
With circular needle, cast on 64 (72) sts. Join, taking care not to twist sts on needle, and pm for beg of rnd.
Set-up rnd *K1, sl 1 p-st with yo; rep from * around.
Rnd 1 *Sl 1 p-st with yo, k next st and yo tog; rep from * around.
Rnd 2 *P next st and yo tog, sl 1 k-st with yo; rep from * around.
Rep rnds 1 and 2 until beanie measures 6½"/16.5cm from beg, end with a rnd 2.

Shape Crown
Note Change to dpn when sts no longer comfortably fit on circular needle.

Place a marker on every 8th (9th) knit rib—4 markers placed.
Next dec rnd [Work in pat to knit rib before marked knit rib, work 2-st decrease] 4 times—8 sts dec'd.
Rep dec rnd every 4th rnd 2 (3) times, then every other rnd once—32 sts.
Work 1 rnd even.
Next dec rnd [Sl 1 p-st with yo, 2-st decrease] 8 times—16 sts.
Cut yarn, pull tail through rem sts, draw up and secure.

FINISHING
Weave in ends. Block to measurements.•

Textured Ribbing Hat

Intermediate

MATERIALS

Yarn (4)
• 3½oz/100g, 218yd/199m of any worsted weight wool in Purple (MC) and Violet (CC)

Needles
• One size 7 (4.5mm) circular needle, 16"/40cm long, *or size to obtain gauge*
• One set (5) size 7 (4.5mm) double-pointed needles (dpn)

Notions
• Stitch marker

MEASUREMENTS
Brim circumference 20"/51cm
Length 9"/23cm

GAUGE
23 sts and 29 rnds to 4"/10cm over stitch pat, slightly stretched, using size 7 (4.5mm) needles.
TAKE TIME TO CHECK YOUR GAUGE.

STITCH PATTERN
Rnd 1 With CC, knit.
Rnd 2 With CC, purl.
Rnd 3 With MC, knit.
Rnd 4–7 With MC, *k1, p1; rep from * around.
Rnds 8–11 With MC, *p1, k1; rep from * around.
Rep rnds 1–11 for stitch pat.

HAT
With circular needle and CC, loosely cast on 116 sts. Join, taking care not to twist sts, and pm for beg of rnd. Purl 1 rnd. Join MC.
Next rnd With MC, *k1, p1; rep from * around.

Rep last rnd for k1, p1 rib for 2"/5cm.
Work rnds 1–11 of stitch pat twice.
With CC, knit 1 rnd, purl 1 rnd.
With MC, knit 1 rnd.
Next rnd With MC, *k1, p1; rep from * to end.
Work rnds 1–11 of stitch pat twice.

Shape Crown
Note Change to dpn when sts no longer fit comfortably on circular needle.
Rnd 1 With CC, *ssk, k2; rep from * around—87 sts.
Rnd 2 With CC, purl.
Rnd 3 With MC, *k2tog, k1; rep from * around—58 sts.
Rnd 4 With MC, *k1, p1; rep from * around.

Rnd 5 With CC, *ssk; rep from * to last 2 sts, k2—30 sts.
Rnd 6 With CC, purl.
Rnd 7 With MC, k3tog, *ssk; rep from * to last 3 sts, k3tog—14 sts.
Rnd 8 With MC, *k1, p1; rep from * around.
Rnd 9 With CC, *ssk; rep from * around—7 sts.
Rnd 10 With CC, purl.
Cut yarn, pull tail through rem sts, draw up and secure.

FINISHING
Weave in ends. Block to measurements. With CC, make a 3"/7.5cm pompom and secure to top of hat.•

Lazy Stripes Hat

MATERIALS

Yarn ③
- 3½oz/100g, 228yd/208m of any DK weight wool yarn in Blue (MC)
- 1¾oz/50g, 114yd/104m of any DK weight wool yarn in Green (CC)

Needles
- One pair size 6 (4mm) needles, *or size to obtain gauge*

MEASUREMENTS

Head circumference 21"/53cm
Length 10¾"/27cm

GAUGE

22 sts and 32 rows to 4"/10cm over St st using size 6 (4mm) needles.
TAKE TIME TO CHECK YOUR GAUGE.

HAT

Beg at the lower edge with CC, cast on 118 sts. Cut CC.
Row 1 (RS) With MC, k2, *p2, k2; rep from * to end.
Row 2 With MC, p2, *k2, p2; rep from * to end.
Rep rows 1 and 2 for k2, p2 rib for 10 rows more.

Begin Stripe Pattern

Row 1 (RS) With CC, knit.
Row 2 With CC, purl.
Rows 3, 5, 7, and 9 With MC, knit.
Row 4, 6, 8, and 10 With MC, purl.
Rep rows 1–10 for stripe pat until piece measures 9"/23cm from beg, end with a stripe row 6.

Shape Crown

Cont to work in the established stripe pat, work as foll:
Dec row 1 (RS) [K11, ssk] 9 times, k1—109 sts.
Row 2 and all WS rows Purl.
Dec row 3 [K10, ssk] 9 times, k1—100 sts.
Dec row 5 [K9, ssk] 9 times, k1—91 sts.
Dec row 7 [K8, ssk] 9 times, k1—82 sts.
Dec row 9 [K7, ssk] 9 times, k1—73 sts.
Dec row 11 [K6, ssk] 9 times, k1—64 sts.
Dec row 13 [K5, ssk] 9 times, k1—55 sts.
Dec row 15 [K4, ssk] 9 times, k1—46 sts.
Cut yarn, pull tail through rem sts twice, draw up and secure.
Sew back seam.

FINISHING

Weave in ends. Block to measurements. With CC, make a 2½"/6.5cm pompom and secure to top of hat.●